I0447906

# Israel Committed Genocide...! Really?

## THE ACCUSATIONS AND WHY THEY ARE WRONG

## Jack Frank Sigman

Copyright © 2016 Jack Frank Sigman

All rights reserved.

ISBN: 1539985997

ISBN 13: 9781539985990

Library of Congress Control Number: 2016919195

CreateSpace Independent Publishing Platform

North Charleston, South Carolina

# Dedication:

*To Janet Nislow Sigman, my one and only.*

# Table of Contents

# Preface

The political movement to de-legitimize Israel has been in full swing for many years. The vaguely antisemitic (to some not vague at all), and definitely anti-Israel, Boycott, Divest, and Sanction (BDS) campaign unofficially came into being 14 years ago with the scholastically impoverished boycott of Israel in 2002 (Docker 2003). Even Norman Finkelstein, no friend to the pro-Israel movement, has stated that the obvious goal of BDS is the de-legitimization of the state of Israel with the finale being Israel's destruction (Smith 2015). While a state can no more, in reality, undergo de-legitimization than a human can be dehumanized, it is the perception of de-legitimization that is the issue at hand. Presently, there are three concepts being used in this illegitimate attempt to delegitimize Israel. Asaf Romirowsky and Efriam Karsh, noted historians and Middle East experts, state those concepts:

1. Demonization of the Jewish state by using the symbols and images associated with classic anti-Semitism to characterize Israel or Israelis; drawing comparisons of contemporary Israeli policy to that of the Nazis; and blaming Israel for all inter-religious or political tensions.
2. Double Standard for Israel by requiring of it a behavior not expected or demanded of any other democratic nation.
3. Delegitimizing Israel by denying the Jewish people its right to self-determination, and denying Israel the right to exist. (Romirowsky and Karsh 2015)

Additional political attacks along the same vein suggest that Israel is an apartheid state, as defined by the United Nations, not as a duplicate of South African Apartheid, but intended as such so that the perception is that the Israeli brand is as bad or significantly worse than the unparalleled apartheid system in South Africa, that the Jews have no historic connection to the Temple Mount (Post 2015), and that Israel was illegitimately born via the commission of genocide. Of course, this is a brand of "political" antisemitism. But none is potentially more damaging politically than the charge of genocide, as Professor Martin Shaw points out, "If the Nakba constituted genocide, then the Palestinian advocates could then trade off 'their' genocide story against Israel's own (narrative)…" (Shaw 2010, 2).

A recent addition to the anti-Israel chorus is the "Black Lives Matters (BLM)" movement coalition named the Movement for Black Lives. They have weighed in with their manifesto, published in 2016 and currently available on their website https://policy.m4bl.org. Their "Invest-Divest" section mentions Israel 11 times. It states that "The US… with Israel and is complicit in the genocide taking place against the Palestinian people." The section also states that "Israel is an apartheid state…." The end goal appears to be ending military aid sent to Israel and other unnamed states that have any human rights violations, which are most state on Earth including the US. Additionally, they want to end individual US states ability to write anti-BDS (the antisemitic movement that seeks to boycott, divest, and sanction Israel until it no longer exists as a Jewish state) legislation, and to join in solidarity with South Africa and Columbia (both major human rights violators) and liberation movements around the world in solidarity (Ndugga-Kabuye and Gilmer 2016). Why Israel is the only state mentioned with a call for discriminatory practices against it is not puzzling. The American Palestinian solidarity umbrella group has been in the forefront attempting to link the current African American – Police Violence controversy with the Palestinian cause. As it appears they have succeeded, this is the most immediate reason for writing this book; to dispel any thought that Israel has ever committed genocide.

While this book is short, in reality it does not take reams of material to prove whether or not Israel has committed the "crime of crimes," the most heinous crime imaginable – Genocide. Further, it should also take little to show that the vast majority of the accusations of genocide are agenda driven, political in nature, and factually bankrupt. While there are a few who, going through the same motions as earlier religious scholars attempting to find out how many angels could dance on a pinhead, legitimately seek to revise Lemkin's definition utilizing his papers. For the majority of accusers, it is only through the use of the style of historical writing advocated by Hayden White, rejected by mainstream historians, that events happen outside of history (Guttenplan 2010, 228), that non-historians can make such genocidal claims.

As an aside, the reader will find various spellings of the words "anti-semite" and "antisemitism." Where I quote another who hyphenates the words, I have no choice in the spelling. However, where it is my writings, I do not hyphenate as I follow the reasoning that the word does not connote hatred of anyone who speaks a Semitic tongue or who has a Semitic background, but anyone who is a Jew, and the original word itself, coined in Germany, is not hyphenated.

As always. I am indebted to my wonderful wife, Janet Nislow Sigman, who made sure I was saying what I wanted to say properly, and whose love and support made this endeavor possible. I am also indebted to Dr. Laurie J. Kemp, Ed.D., who provided excellent editorial direction, Dr. Paul Bartrop, Ph.D. and Eve Grimm, Esq., for their sage advice, and Giles Raymond DeMourot, for his all-around wisdom and first hand historical knowledge – because he was there.

Strangely, I am also indebted to Professors Francis A. Boyle, John Docker, and Richard Falk, for without their almost fanatical scholarly attempts to try to prove Israel committed and continues to commit genocide, the original need to write this book would never have come about.

# Introduction

From the folding's of its robe, it brought two children; wretched, abject, frightful, hideous, miserable. They knelt down at its feet, and clung upon the outside of its garment.

"Oh, Man, look here! Look, look, down here!" exclaimed the Ghost.

They were a boy and a girl. Yellow, meagre, ragged, scowling, wolfish; but prostrate, too, in their humility. Where graceful youth should have filled their features out, and touched them with its freshest tints, a stale and shriveled hand, like that of age, had pinched, and twisted them, and pulled them into shreds. Where angels might have sat enthroned, devils lurked, and glared out menacing. No change, no degradation, no perversion of humanity, in any grade, through all the mysteries of wonderful creation, has monsters half so horrible and dread.

Scrooge started back, appalled. Having them shown to him in this way, he tried to say they were fine children, but the words choked themselves, rather than be parties to a lie of such enormous magnitude.

"Spirit, are they yours?" Scrooge could say no more.

"They are Man's," said the Spirit, looking down upon them. "And they cling to me, appealing from their fathers. This boy is Ignorance. This girl is Want. Beware them both, and all of their degree, but most of all beware this boy, for on his brow I see that written which is Doom, unless the writing be erased. Deny it!" cried the Spirit, stretching out its hand towards the city. "Slander those who tell it ye. Admit it for your factious purposes, and make it worse. And abide the end." (Dickens 1843)

Ilan Pappé, in his book *The Ethnic Cleansing of Israel*, professes that it is his understanding, based on the Israeli archives he has read, that the nascent Jewish leadership, of the soon to be established Israeli Defense Force, planned to remove all Arab presence from what would become the Jewish state of Israel. While Pappé maintains that the thought of Arab displacement was always a part of Zionist aspirations, he claims it first became active policy as retaliation for Palestinian attacks in early 1947 and was later expanded, via formal plan, in March of 1948, as a call to forcibly move the entirety of the Palestinian Arab population to anywhere outside of British Mandate Palestine.

Referred to as "Plan Dalet," Pappé states that such a plan would be considered a crime against humanity today (Pappé 2006a, xii-xiii). Of course there is no reason why, today, it would not be considered a crime against humanity. However, considering all of the similar episodes of wholesale removal of an unwanted population, especially when deemed to be a physical danger to the state, such an act was not considered a crime against humanity. Additionally, as Plan Dalet was not a plan to remove the Arab population out of British Mandate Palestine, no crime as such was committed.

When the scale of fatalities vs. the number of people moved during this conflict is compared to actual episodes of ethnic cleansing committed before and after it, perhaps this episode should merely be considered a "misdemeanor against humanity." But, in accordance with the UNGA Convention on the Prevention and Punishment of the Crime of Genocide, can it be deemed genocide?

During my educational journey toward my graduate degree in international relations, I noted the numerous case studies concerning post-World War II (WW II) states whose independence were preceded by an act of genocide (or what appeared to be genocide) visited upon them either by a colonial power or by the original state from which they were attempting to secede. This group of states includes Kosovo, Bangladesh, and East Timor. However, there are other groups that have undergone similar genocidal episodes, such as the Chechens (from Russia) and the Tamils (from Sri Lanka) who appear nowhere close to independence. A comparative study of the historical record of these case studies was the basis for my Master's thesis; that for an independence movement to succeed post-WWII, it appears they must undergo an act of genocide, or close enough to resemble genocide, in order to generate sufficient world sympathy and indignation to force the opposition to grant state independence. But there is a caveat; the candidate state must not have committed an equally, if not worse, heinous crime against their "oppressor."

Like the Chechens and the Tamils, there is a group that has been seeking independence for the last 98/67/48 (depending on the various interpretations of nationalism) years; the Arabs of the Palestinian region, known today as the Palestinians, although for many years before 1948, when one spoke of a Palestinian, they were likely referring to a Jew and not an Arab (Goldberg 2005, 230). Even though they were supposed to attain their independence in 1948, via United Nation General Assembly (UNGA) Resolution 181 (II) partitioning British Mandate Palestine into separate Jewish and Arab states, their seeming inability to build community support, matched with the refusal to form any viable government agencies, along with the initiation of the Palestinian Civil War (1947-48), as well as joining in the subsequent first Arab-Israel War (1948-49), resulted in Arab Palestinian independence being "strangled" (R. Khalidi 2001, 17-21).

From 1949 through 1967, the vast majority of Palestinians lived under Jordanian, Egyptian, Lebanese, or Syrian rule. Jordan (formerly Transjordan until renamed after the British and Pakistani recognized annexation of the west bank of the Jordan River, known as the hill country of Samaria and Judea in both the pre-1949 Palestinian region and the UNGA Partition Resolution 181) annexed the remaining portion of British Mandate Palestine, including the old portion of Jerusalem, east of Israel, and granted the Palestinians living there Jordanian citizenship. Egypt took military and administrative control of Gaza but did not annex it. Other major Palestinian refugee centers exist in Syria, Lebanon, and Egypt; the states (along with Jordan) that border Israel.

In 1967, the Jordanian and Egyptian controlled portions of the former British Mandate Palestine parcels of land, plus the Syrian Golan Heights And Egyptian Sinai Peninsula, along with their populations, came under the military control of Israel. This was the end result of the Jordanian, Syrian, and Egyptian troops being driven out of those territories during the Six Day Arab-Israeli War. Israel then annexed the Golan Heights and the portion of Jerusalem they did not previously control, including the "old" city (Tessler 2009, 399).

At that time, possibly due to the prospect of rule by Jews, as well as the now lessened influence of Jordan and Egypt (Bickerton 2010, 156-7), the largely Islamic Palestinian population quickly expanded their nascent nationalism into an actual struggle for independence (Tessler 2009, 429), instead of merely haphazardly working to "liberate Palestine" in order to return the entirety of the land to Islamic rule (Tessler 2009, 275). Those previous struggles failed because they were either lackluster (Said 2001) or were so overly violent they were discounted by a majority of the influential members of the international community.

However, in the last few decades, it appears that the Palestinians and their supporters are trying to superficially adopt the strategies and tactics of successful independence and revolutionary movements, in the attempt to generate a critical mass of international sympathy which in turn will cause a majority to actively support Palestinian independence. These ploys include; acting as victims of an oppressive colonial power, likening themselves to Native Americans invaded by a European power; imagining themselves as indigenous South Africans, again subjected by European colonial powers who have instituted a system of Apartheid to maintain white political control; claiming that, morally, the Palestinian Nakba is equivalent to the Holocaust, and going so far as to claim "Nakba denial" as a crime against humanity. The ultimate claim is that the Jews committed genocide during the 1947-49 Palestinian Civil War/Arab-Israeli war, and that rather than seeing the image of the Jewish people regaining independence in their homeland while rising out of the ashes of the Nazi Holocaust, what should be seen is an image of Israel rising out of a Jewish-initiated holocaust of the innocent and peaceful Palestinian people. The Palestinians up that claim to the accusation that genocide continues through today.

In the first chapter of "Denying the Holocaust," noted Holocaust historian Deborah Lipstadt discusses the logic pertaining to her refusal to appear on stage, or on the news, if the purpose of the appearance is to debate Holocaust deniers. Her rationale for steering clear of such encounters is that such activity tends to elevate "denial ideology" and portends that Holocaust deniers have a side worth anyone listening to, that Holocaust deniers might be legitimate researchers and scholars, thus having a legitimate point of view (Lipstadt 1993, 1-3).

In that same manner, this book is not written to be an open stage for a debate. No genocide accusers have been invited to contribute chapters. And while their works will grace the pages of this book, it will be solely for the purpose of pointing out the absurdity of their claims when taken in context. As stated by Canadian attorney Trevor Sher:

> It may be that some people find something darkly poetic in the idea that the Jews, who suffered one of the most horrible tragedies in history, are now inflicting that same horror against someone else. But Nietzscheism aside, it takes only a modicum of scrutiny (if that) to understand that the comparison of today's Jewish state to yesterday's Nazi regime is not only false, but also a targeted political strategy – and a disgustingly anti-Semitic one at that – which is being exploited in order to turn the Jewish people's saddest and most horrifying moment in history against them. (Sher 2015)

Samuel Katz, a member of the first Israeli Knesset, stated that "many people throughout the world... are prepared at the slightest provocation to pontificate on the Israeli-Arab conflict hav(ing) never troubled to check the veracity of the information by which they are presumably convinced" (Katz 2002, xi).

Keep that in mind when you reread the introduction's opening passage wherein Charles Dickens, the noted 19th century author and moralist, warns us of the folly of willful ignorance buttressing actual ignorance. It is my contention that any who advocates the charge that Israel committed genocide, or considers committing genocide, is willfully ignorant, and they are guilty of trying to influence a multitude of those who are just plain ignorant. In the immortal words of Emile Zola in his literary attack in the defense of Alfred Dreyfus against the French courts; *J'Accuse.*

# Chapter One

# The Second Russell Tribunal on Palestine (2014)

There have been many "international people's tribunals" convened over the last 80 years. The first, a "people's investigation" into the German Reichstag's burning in 1933, was invoked to upstage, and thus thwart the Nazi's planned show trial of communists (Jones 2006, 376). The most visible tribunal was likely the Bertrand Russell Vietnam War Crimes Tribunal of 1967, which was an "International War Tribunal" set to judge the United States over its conduct in Vietnam. Other tribunals have dealt with wars on women, wars on indigenous people, economic wars on poor states, and various accusations of illegal war and genocide (Jones 2006, 375).

For the most part, these tribunals, which attempt to substitute public humiliation for lawful process and punishment, are considered little more than kangaroo courts with preordained verdicts. Regardless, they do "make some contribution to the pathetically limited possibilities of action for the punishment of genocide" (Jones 2006, 376). However, this is a two-edged sword because agenda-driven radical groups can deliberately misuse the moral value of such "peoples" justice to accuse states of crimes that were simply not committed. The Second Russell Tribunal on Palestine is certainly such a case of inappropriate justice.

The First Russell Tribunal on Palestine was established in 2009 by the Bertrand Russel Peace Foundation. As relayed by NGO Monitor:

> With no judicial basis, the RToP uses a legal façade to create an image of neutrality and credibility. The sessions

have "jurors" examining expert "witnesses," and the "findings" are then published. The use of legal terms and concepts such as "witnesses" and "jurors" belies the complete lack of legal legitimacy and basic notions of impartiality and fairness integral to any legal proceedings. (NGO Monitor 2012)

That Tribunal was held in 4 separate states over a period of three years, 2010 through 2012. The first session, held in Barcelona, dealt with European complicity in Israel's "occupation" of the (disputed) Palestinian territories. The second session was held in London and dealt with the international community's complicity in Israel's "violations" of Palestinian human rights. The third session, held in Cape Town, dealt with determining if Israel's behavior toward the Palestinians is worse than South Africa's Apartheid regime. The fourth session was held in New York City and considered the United States' and the UN's complicity in Israel's "violations" of international law (NGO Monitor 2012). The Second Russel Tribunal on Palestine was held in Brussels in 2014 wherein Israel's actions during the 2014 excursion into Gaza, called "Protective Edge," were considered.

In September of 2014, Stephen Lendman, a Harvard and Wharton educated economist, writing in *Rense*, stated that Israel was found guilty of "Genocidal High Crimes." Lendman, who is also a contributor to *Veteran's Today* and is the host of the *Progressive News Hour* (This is a pejorative reference, not a positive attribute. *Veteran's Today* is considered by many to be a well-produced disinformation website that runs anti-semitic, extremist viewpoints and conspiracy theories (ADL 2015)), referenced the "Second Russell Tribunal on Palestine" as his source of information. He claims the tribunal found that Israel's "forces committed the highest of genocidal high crimes against peace." (Lendman 2014). "High Crimes" as in "high crimes and misdemeanors" refers to those punishable offenses that only apply to high persons, that is, to public officials, those who, because of their official status, are under special obligations that ordinary persons are not under, and which could not be meaningfully applied or justly punished if committed by ordinary persons. Therefore, referring to such as the "highest" of high crimes indicates that it is the head of state, the prime minister of Israel, who is inciting genocide. The following information should prove that Lendman has no idea what he is writing about, or if he does, he is deliberately distorting the facts for an audience that wants to believe that Israel is committing genocide. This is not the first time Lendman has made such allegations (Lendman 2011).

The major problem with Lendman's accusation is that the Russell Tribunal did not find Israel guilty of the crime of genocide. The Tribunal did not find that Israel's forces committed any genocidal crimes. While Israeli actions were examined to determine if Israel had committed genocide, based on both the legal definition and on "broader understandings of genocide beyond that defined for the purposes of individual criminal responsibility...," no act of genocide was found. What the Second Russell Tribunal on Palestine did find was that it could be convolutedly construed that there was incitement for genocide made by a few public and political figures within Israel, and that Israeli officials failed to follow the proscription of the Genocide Convention in that "individuals who attempt or who incite to genocide 'shall be punished, whether they are constitutionally responsible rulers, public officials or private individuals'" (RToP 2014, 10). Regardless, it does not appear that any state at any time has ever followed the proscription of the Genocide Convention concerning political speech that borders on the incitement to commit genocide. It is certain that no Arab or Islamic state has ever made such a charge against its officials when the target of genocidal incitement is Israel.

Of course, acting on the ruling set forth by the judges of the Tribunal requires following the Russell Tribunal's line of reasoning by the Israeli authorities responsible for charging, coming to the same understanding, that the comments made by those mentioned "high officials" were made with the intent to encourage genocidal behavior. In order for the Israeli officials to come to that construed opinion requires them to adopt the same mindset as the jurors of the Russell Tribunal. Having that transformational mindset is neither likely nor reasonable to expect.

Those jurors were; International Law Professor and former special rapporteur for the UN Commission on Human Rights and International Law Commission John Dugard; lawyer Michael Mansfield; UN Human Rights Council Special Rapporteur for Palestine Richard Falk, who considered the original Russell tribunal "a juridical farce" (Jones 2006, 376); Pink Floyd band founding member Roger Waters; novelist, and political and cultural commentator Ahdaf Soueif; former South African government minister, activist, and writer Ronald Kasrils; anti-globalization and environmental activist Vandana Shiva; film and television director Ken Loach; lawyer and script writer Paul Laverty; activist and author Christianne Hessel; human rights lawyer Radhia Nasraoui; and pianist and UNESCO goodwill ambassador Miguel Angel Estrella. Few had any legal training and none of them are particularly noted for their legal expertise in the Israeli/Palestinian conflict, other than Richard Falk, who condemned the original Russell Tribunal as a judicial farce, and John Dugard, Falk's immediate predecessor as chief anti-Israel agitator at the UNHRC. Both Falk and Dugard have been condemned at the UN for their comments concerning Israel. Falk, in particular, has been singled out by numerous UN officials and Ambassadors for his inability to be professionally objective when it comes to the subject of Israel as well as having posted anti-semitic material (UNHRC 2006) (Charbonneau 2014).

To say that the jurors on the Russell Tribunal were biased, and for the most part inadequately educated to act as judges, would likely be an understatement. Indeed, based on the composition of the pool of judges, there seemed not one who might have looked favorably on Israel, had there been any witnesses who might have been there to defend Israel's actions. Of course there were no such witnesses. After all, when a lawful court with qualified legal minds convened to render judgment on the legality of the Israeli Separation Barrier, the barrier that reduced the number of suicide bombings in Israel to zero, the International Court of Justice gave no credence to Israel's explanation as to the reason for constructing the Security Barrier (McGreal 2004). Therefore, why would any supporter of Israel believe that a court comprised of the judges of the Russell

Tribunal would give any credence to Israel's justification for its defense against Hamas rocket fire?

Richard Falk, in his own article explaining the declaration of the judges, stated that, "It should be acknowledged that this undertaking was never intended to be a neutral inquiry without any predispositions" (Falk 2014). Further, Falk explains that Israel is not even legally allowed to defend itself because "the claim of self-defense does not exist in relation to resistance mounted by an occupied people, and Gaza from the perspective of international law remains occupied due to Israeli persisting effective control despite Israel's purported disengagement in 2005" (Falk 2014).

The witness list, those who testified in front of the Russell Tribunal, was also provided by Lendman; Palestinian Center for Human Rights director Raji Sourani; Economics editor Paul Mason; Mohammed Omer; Physicians Mohammad Abou-Arab and Mads Gilbert; European Palestinian BDS national committee coordinator Michael Deas; and Journalists Max Blumenthal, David Sheen, and Martin Lejeune; Defense for Children International-Palestine advocacy unit coordinator Ivan Karakashian; Israeli investigative researcher and former IDF soldier Paul Behrens; Independent journalist and filmmaker David Sheen; arms expert Col. Desmond Travers; Gazan filmmaker Ashraf Mashharawi; and the Aprodev Advocacy for just Peace in Palestine official Agnes Bertrand. Their commonality is that they all have a specific dog in the fight against Israel.

Who was there for the defense of Israel? No one. Again, what would be the purpose of bothering to show up for the defense of Israel with the tin-plated list of jurors whose main commonality is their hatred and activism against Israel?

The question still remains; why even bother to attempt to try Israel on a charge of genocide? A podcast discussion by Joshua Oppenheimer and David Rief about the international community's reaction to genocide might provide a partial answer. According to Oppenheimer and Rief, there is a need to get worked up through righteous indignation in order to consider intervention in a regional or intrastate affair (FP Staff 2015). It would then appear that the mindset of the proponents of the Russell Tribunal on Palestine is to do whatever is required to make the international community reach that level of indignation.

Oppenheimer takes this further in an analogy with his concept of the "Bush Doctrine":

> When the society becomes indignant, it can become hubristic. I think that indignation is pleasurable, and it's pleasurable because it's self-righteous. And, of course, the follies of the Blair and Bush interventions were all about this false sense of: "We're good, and now all we have to do is identify the good guys in every country and support them and then everything we do should be good." The world becomes kind of distorted and obscured by this false moral view of oneself. (FP Staff 2015)

It is that false moral view that is being cultivated by the Russell Tribunal's "judges." If they can convince the world that Israel committed genocide, then it should be relatively easy to convince the international community to intervene.

And there is more. Stephen Carter, a Yale law professor, discusses the atrocities allegedly committed by the Allies against the Germans during WW II. Carter brings up the issue regarding the 1989 international best-seller by James Bacque, *Other Losses*, which detailed the deaths of upwards of one million German prisoners of war due to the actions of the Allied Powers during WW II. Scholarly critics savaged the book as a product of poor research practices, but the damage to the reputations of the Allied Powers was done. So despite the eventual knowledge that the "facts" were wildly exaggerated events, the US lost a great deal of moral stature. Why so? Because there are forces in the world that want to believe those fallacious and exaggerated tales of events that occurred more than 40 years earlier, while fighting a war against an almost absolute immoral power, are true, which would make those western liberal democracies just as immoral (Carter 2011, 97-98).

The same affect took hold when Daniel Goldhagen published *Hitler's Willing Executioners*. People wanted to believe there was something inherently wrong with Germans, which would have been a neat and simple explanation as to how the Holocaust could have happened, rather than having to deal with the notion that Woody Allen is correct when he quipped about the Holocaust in *Hannah and Her Sisters*:

> "And more puzzled intellectuals declaring their mystification over the systematic murder of millions. The reason they can never answer the question "How could it possibly happen?" is that it's the wrong question. Given what people are, the question is "Why doesn't it happen more often?" (Frederick 1986)

Therefore, it is possible that the ultimate reason for the Russell Tribunal's attack on Israel is an attempt to destroy Israel's well-deserved reputation for behavior as moral as humanly possible in time of war, given the situation and circumstances, often extreme, and the conduct of individual troops under high stress. Of course, we will always have Orwell to guide us when these accusations surface; "Atrocities are believed in, or disbelieved in, solely on the grounds of political predilection" (Carter 2011, 98).

# Chapter Two

# What is Genocide?

Deborah Lipstadt, in *Denying the Holocaust*, expounds on the conduct of academics on American campuses. She discusses encounters with college professors who throw in Holocaust denial literature as factual counterparts to the standard, peer reviewed, historical texts and articles on the Holocaust. She wonders why and if a professor's responsibility "to maintain some fidelity to the notion of truth" has been supplanted by the "American Ideal of Fairness" in the notion that everyone has the right to speak his/her piece and be allowed to be believed as if they were speaking the truth. (Lipstadt 1993, 3)

Interestingly, the one noted academic who has unwittingly lent his reputation to the Holocaust deniers is Noam Chomsky. Chomsky, cited within the field of Arts and Humanities more often than any other living scholar between 1980 and 1992, is often referred to as the "leading living public intellectual" (Rochester 2015). However, his star was more than slightly tarnished when he agreed to allow the use of an essay he wrote as the introduction to a Holocaust denial text written by Robert Faurisson (Jochnowitz ND). While Chomsky's essay dealt with "freedom of speech," the connection of his name with Faurisson's lent an air of undeserved respectability to Faurisson's work, which is far more related to propaganda than research.

Regardless, unlike those who claim Israel has committed genocide, Holocaust deniers have no scholars of note within their movement. The last pretender to such scholarship, the self-taught historian David Irving, hoisted himself on his own petard when he sued Professor Lipstadt and her publisher for libel. He was upset that he was pointed out as a particularly potent Holocaust denier in Lipstadt's book *Denying the Holocaust* (HDOT 2013). Five years and millions of dollars later, the trial ended with Irving being branded as both an antisemite and a Holocaust denier by the trial judge. But that was not the end of the story.

Incredulously, the British court was taken to task by two noted historians, Donald Cameron Watt and Sir John Keegan. Their separate published complaints dealt with their worries that anyone should hold David Irving, or any historian, to such high standards of truth. Neither discussed the fact that Irving sued to protect a reputation that he did not actually deserve and that Lipstadt was the scholar being brought to task to prove her previously proven identification of Irving as a Holocaust denier. No one knows what purpose those two historians served when they came to Irving's belated defense. However, Ian Buruma has a possible reason for such defense:

> People on the left, no less than extreme right-wingers, are quick to suspect conspiracies, and tend to look for hidden proof, preferably in obscure documents, that would unmask the conspirators and make the powerful look foolish. This is why left-wing radicals are often the first to leap to the defense of extremists whose opinions are threatened with censorship, even if they don't share them. (Buruma 2001)

### What is Genocide?

Amazingly, whenever genocide is to be discussed, scholars never seem to tire of reproducing the official document, United Nation General Assembly (UNGA) resolution 1021, the Convention on the Prevention and Punishment of the Crime of Genocide, wherein article II, sections a through e, list the various acts, and article III, sections a through e, list the various punishable acts with the caveat that the acts must be committed with the intent to commit them (UNGA 1948). In this matter of commission, it is an absolute fact that there can be no such thing as an accidental genocide or genocide by misadventure. The resolution was approved on December 9, 1948 and came into force on January 12, 1951.

However, it appears rare that the earlier UNGA resolution, the one that deals with declaring genocide a crime, is rarely, if ever, produced. UNGA Resolution 96i, one of the very first UNGA resolutions, passed on December 11, 1946, nearly two years prior to the Genocide Convention. This is the definition of genocide in use at that time:

> Genocide is a denial of the right of existence of entire human groups, as homicide is the denial of the right to live of individual human beings; such denial of the right of existence shocks the conscience of mankind, results in great losses to humanity in the form of cultural and other contributions represented by these human groups, and is contrary to moral law and to the spirit and aims of the United Nations.
>
> Many instances of such crimes of genocide have occurred when racial, religious, political, and other groups have been destroyed, entirely or in part. (UNGA 1946)

Combining the definition of genocide as imparted by the 1946 resolution with the numeration of the acts that compose the crime, it is clear that genocide is the intentional murder or attempted murder of entire groups which would entail significant losses; losses so great as to shock the conscience of mankind. As a writer for the Huffington Post once said, "People tend to misuse the word 'genocide,' because it is the only common term we have to describe unimaginable slaughter" (Cooper 2011a).

There are other definitions of genocide developed by numerous recognized scholars. However, just as many scholars disagree over the conventional definitions. As tersely stated by genocide scholar Hannibal Travis, "Genocide is a far more controversial term" (Travis 2013, 21).

The word "genocide" was coined by Raphael Lemkin, a Polish attorney of international law, who had long sought international organizational recognition of such crimes; first, in 1933, through petition to the League of Nations to recognize crimes of barbarity and vandalism as new offenses against the law of nations, and later as the Genocide Convention enacted by the UN in 1948 (Docker 2010, 50).

That convention, The UN Genocide Convention on the Prevention and Punishment of Genocide, defines genocide as follows:

> In the present Convention, genocide means any of the following acts committed with the intent to destroy, in whole or in part, a national, ethnical, racial, or religious group, as such:
>
> a. Killing members of the group.
> b. Causing serious bodily or mental harm to members of the group.
> c. Deliberately inflicting on the group conditions of life calculated to bring about its physical destruction in whole or in part.
> d. Imposing measures intended to prevent births within the group.
> e. Forcibly transferring children of the group to another group. (UNGA 1948)

However, as Kuper points out in his introduction to the reports of the discussions held by the individual members of the Convention:

> It was a complete delusion to suppose that the adoption of a convention of the type proposed, even if general adhered to, would give people a greater sense of security or would diminish existing dangers of persecution on racial, religious or national grounds (Kuper 1982, 19).

Lemkin's definition of genocide indicates that there is a "coordinated plan of different actions aimed at the destruction of the essential foundations of life of a group" which indicates intent (Docker 2010, 50). A

UN commission, examining the crisis in Darfur, determined that to be genocidal, the planners must have had the intent to murder the entire targeted group (Travis 2013, 21). French law takes a more liberal view, stating that genocide can be any of the above acts committed against *any* identifiable group, despite not being a national, ethnical, racial, or religious group.

### *Various scholarly definitions of Genocide*

Adam Jones, in *Genocide: A Comprehensive Introduction*, reputed to be "the most wide-ranging, accessible and clear-sighted introduction to the subject" (Levene 2010), provides a chronological list of various scholarly definitions including those scholars who changed their personal definitions as time went by:

> Peter Drost in 1959: "Genocide is the deliberate destruction of physical life of individual human beings by reason of their membership of any human collectivity as such."
>
> Vahakn Darian in 1975: "Genocide is the successful attempt by a dominant group, vested with formal authority and/or with preponderant access to the overall resources of power, to reduce by coercion or lethal violence the number of a minority group whose ultimate extermination is held desirable and useful and whose respective vulnerability is a major factor contributing to the decision for genocide."
>
> Irving Louis Horowitz in 1976: "[Genocide is] a structural and systematic destruction of innocent people by a state bureaucratic apparatus . . . Genocide represents a systematic effort over time to liquidate a national population, usually a minority . . . [and] functions as a fundamental political policy to assure conformity and participation of the citizenry."
>
> Leo Kuper in 1981: "I shall follow the definition of genocide given in the [UN] Convention. This is not to say that I

agree with the definition. On the contrary, I believe a major omission to be in the exclusion of political groups from the list of groups protected. In the contemporary world, political differences are at the very least as significant a basis for massacre and annihilation as racial, national, ethnic or religious differences.

Then too, the genocides against racial, national, ethnic or religious groups are generally a consequence of, or intimately related to, political conflict. However, I do not think it helpful to create new definitions of genocide, when there is an internationally recognized definition and a Genocide Convention which might become the basis for some effective action, however limited the underlying conception. But since it would vitiate the analysis to exclude political groups, I shall refer freely . . . to liquidating or exterminatory actions against them."

Jack Porter in 1982: "Genocide is the deliberate destruction, in whole or in part, by a government or its agents, of a racial, sexual, religious, tribal or political minority. It can involve not only mass murder, but also starvation, forced deportation, and political, economic and biological subjugation. Genocide involves three major components: ideology, technology, and bureaucracy/organization."

Isidor Wallimann and Michael N. Dobkowski in 1983: "Genocide is the deliberate, organized destruction, in whole or in large part, of racial or ethnic groups by a government or its agents. It can involve not only mass murder, but also forced deportation (ethnic cleansing), systematic rape, and economic and biological subjugation."

Henry Huttenbach in 1988: "Genocide is any act that puts the very existence of a group in jeopardy."

Helen Fein in 1988: "Genocide is a series of purposeful actions by a perpetrator(s) to destroy a collectivity through mass or selective murders of group members and suppressing the biological and social reproduction of the collectivity. This can be accomplished through the imposed proscription or restriction of reproduction of group members, increasing infant mortality, and breaking the linkage between reproduction and socialization of children in the family or group of origin. The perpetrator may represent the state of the victim, another state, or another collectivity.

Frank Chalk and Kurt Jonassohn in 1990: "Genocide is a form of one-sided mass killing in which a state or other authority intends to destroy a group, as that group and membership in it are defined by the perpetrator.

Helen Fein in 1993 (5 years after her first definition) "Genocide is sustained purposeful action by a perpetrator to physically destroy a collectivity directly or indirectly, through interdiction of the biological and social reproduction of group members, sustained regardless of the surrender or lack of threat offered by the victim.

Steven Katz in 1994: [Genocide is] the actualization of the intent, however successfully carried out, to murder in its totality (Modified by Adam Jones in 2010 to read, "murder in whole or in part. . . .") any national, ethnic, racial, religious, political, social, gender or economic group, as these groups are defined by the perpetrator, by whatever means" (Modified by Adam Jones in 2010 to read, "murder in whole or in part. . . .".

Israel Charney in 1994: Genocide in the generic sense means the mass killing of substantial numbers of human beings, when not in the course of military action against the military forces of an avowed enemy, under conditions of the essential defencelessness (sic) of the victim.

Irving Louis Horowitz in 1996 (20 years after his earlier definition): "Genocide is herein defined as a *structural and systematic destruction of innocent people by a state bureaucratic apparatus* [emphasis in original]. . . . Genocide means the physical dismemberment and liquidation of people on large scales, an attempt by those who rule to achieve the total elimination of a subject people" (Horowitz supports "carefully distinguishing the [Jewish] Holocaust from genocide"; he also refers to "the phenomenon of mass murder, for which genocide is a synonym").

Barbara Harff in 2003: "Genocides and politicides are the promotion, execution, and/or implied consent of sustained policies by governing elites or their agents – or, in the case of civil war, either of the contending authorities – that are intended to destroy, in whole or part, a communal, political, or politicized ethnic group (Harff adds that genocidal acts "are never accidental, nor are they the acts of individuals," "...they are carried out at the explicit or tactic direction of state authorities, or from those who claim state authority" Harff 2003, 58).

Manus I. Midlarsk in 2005: "Genocide is understood to be the state-sponsored systematic mass murder of innocent and helpless men, women, and children denoted by a particular ethnoreligious identity, having the purpose of eradicating this group from a particular territory."

Mark Levene in 2005: "Genocide occurs when a state, perceiving the integrity of its agenda to be threatened by an aggregate population – defined by the state as an organic collectivity, or series of collectivities – seeks to remedy the situation by the systematic, *en masse* physical elimination of that aggregate, *in toto*, or until it is no longer perceived to represent a threat."

Jacques Sémelin in 2005: "I will define genocide as that particular process of civilian destruction that is directed at the total eradication of a group, the criteria by which it is identified being determined by the perpetrator."

Daniel Chirot and Clark McCauley in 2006: "A genocidal mass murder is politically motivated violence that
directly or indirectly kills a substantial proportion of a targeted population, combatants and noncombatants alike,
regardless of their age or gender."

Martin Shaw in 2007: "Genocide is a form of violent
social conflict, or war, between armed power organizations that aim to destroy civilian social groups and those
groups and other actors who resist this destruction."

Donald Bloxham in 2009: "[Genocide is] the physical destruction of a large portion of a group in a limited
or unlimited territory with the intention of destroying that
group's collective existence." (Jones 2010)

Colin Tatz in *With Intent to Destroy* also lists a number of scholars' definitions with these not being on Jones' list (Tatz 2003, x-xi):

Steven Katz: The concept of genocide applies only when there is an
actualized intent, however successfully carried out, to physically destroy
and entire group (as such a group is defined by the perpetrators).

Jennifer Balint: Genocide is the sustained purposive action perpetuated by the state, or actors condoned by the state, on a captured victim
group as defined by the perpetrator(s), leading to the physical destruction
of the group – Jennifer Balint

Paul Boghossian, professor of philosophy at NYU explains that genocide,
as a concept, is supposed to be a:

"distinctive phenomenon, something that is not denoted
by any other terms that we already have in the language.
Lemkin believed that in the Jewish and Armenian cases
he had observed a distinctive crime, something that deserved to be called *the murder of a people*, that none of
the other terms at our disposal – as mass murder, for example – denoted.

(Second), it is supposed to name a phenomenon that is, *as part of its very meaning, morally wrong.* Unlike the notion of *killing*, for example, but like the notion of *murder*, it is not supposed to be an open question about any given genocide whether it was morally reprehensible; it's not supposed to be intelligible to ask: Yes it was genocide, but was it justified? It's supposed to analytically from the very meaning of the term that, if it was genocide, it was wrong. (Boghossian 2010, 73)

Even with the dozens of scholarly interpretations of the word genocide, this common sense definition remains; genocide is intentional and state-directed mass death (Docker 2010, 50). While neither accurate nor legal, this is the definition of genocide that likely has the most emotional reaction for the international community. Paul Boghossian echoes that sentiment wherein he reflects that "(g)enocide is taken to name not only a distinctive crime but one that is distinctively heinous, deserving of a special measure of censure. Mass murder may be bad, but mass murder done in the context of the targeting of a particular group is supposed to be morally much worse" (Boghossian, Academia.edu 2015, 3).

Finally, Dirk Moses, a genocide specialist regarding its relationship with colonialism, added his own opinion as to what he understands to be the international community's definition of genocide, while complaining that genocide is so much more. He states:

Consider the definition of genocide used by the current anti-genocide campaign: The International Campaign to End Genocide covers genocide as it is defined in the Genocide Convention: "The intentional destruction, in whole or in part, of a national, ethnical, racial or religious group, as such." It also covers political mass murder, ethnic cleansing, and other genocide-like crimes against humanity. *It will not get bogged down in legal debates during mass killing* (emphasis added).

Yet only one of the five techniques of genocide in the UN definition concerns mass killing. The fact is that leading genocide scholars have taken the Holocaust as the paradigm of genocide despite their ostensible rejection of Holocaust uniqueness. Ignoring or rejecting the capacious definition of Raphael Lemkin, who invented the concept and included non-murderous techniques of genocide, they redefined it as an ideologically-motivated and state-executed program of mass killing (Moses, 2006).

For instance, the prolific author and genocide scholar, Barbara Harff, defined genocide "as a particular form of state terror … mass murder, premeditated by some power-wielding group linked with state power." The background assumption was made explicit in her aside that "The Jewish Holocaust … is employed as the yardstick, the *ultimate criterion* for assessing the scope, methods, targets, and victims of [other] genocides" (Harff 1986, 165).

That the Holocaust is a reference point for many NGOs is readily apparent in a link from the Genocide Intervention Network to the online project Facing History, an anti-racism educational program that promotes "the development of a more humane and informed citizenry" through study of "the historical development and lessons of the Holocaust and other examples of genocide" (Facing History 2015). There did not appear to be any mention on the website of the millions of indigenous peoples who once lived on the North American continent, although one would think that reflecting on their fate would entail an authentic "facing of history.":

The focus of "genocide studies" and NGOs was made explicit by Frank Chalk when he told his readers that "we must never forget that the great genocides of the past have been committed by [state] perpetrators who acted in the name of absolutist or utopian ideologies aimed at cleansing and purifying their worlds"(Chalk, 1994: 58f). "Genocide studies," then, is really a version of totalitarianism theory because by definition a genocide – at least a true one – can only be committed by a totalitarian or at least authoritarian state driven by a utopian ideology. (Moses 2006)

And here is the caveat: In his review of Alexander Laban Hinton's "Genocide: An Anthropological Reader," Dr. Paul Bartrop brings out the complexities dealing with the very meaning and usage of the word:

This is a term (genocide) that today carries much more power than previously, and precision is needed when applying it. The problem is, genocide is actually a number of things, and each requires a distinct methodical approach. It is, in the first place, a crime – for many, "the crime of crimes"; it is a social problem of the first magnitude; it is an academic area of study; and it is a new term in the English language whose full meaning has for many not yet become apparent, leading to its frequent misapplication. Quite clearly, given all this, a number of distinct approaches can not only be taken but must be taken if sense is to be derived from the term. We need to know what it is and what it is not if we are to be effective in employing it in scholarly discourse.

The alternative, a situation in which anything goes and all examples of human evil can be accepted or rejected as genocide according to personal preferences can lead to a debasing of the concept." (Bartrop 2004, 269)

### *Why did the Genocide Convention come into being?*

William Schabas, an eminent genocide scholar, in an interview in 2006, discussed the push for the Genocide Convention as a reaction to the lack of certain charges against the high ranking Nazi officials at the Nuremburg Military Tribunal.

> The Great Powers (US, USSR, Britain, France), at the 1944 meeting of the United Nations War Crimes Commission, organized to investigate the war crimes committed by Nazi Germany, were pressed by NGOs as to the crimes that should be charged regarding the treatment of the Jews and other groups that were citizens of Germany at the time before the war had started, the years between 1933 and 1939. However, those criminal acts were considered internal issues and were not covered by international law at that time. Additionally, those same type crimes, perhaps at a lesser severity but still the same crimes, had been, and were being, committed by the Great Powers to their own state citizens, as well as their subjects in colonial possessions. Not wishing to be the subject of the same charges, they determined that the crime under which the Nazis were eventually charged, crimes against humanity, had to be associated with a war, thus absolving themselves of both moral guilt and legal charge, for the same crimes being committed outside of a war scenario. Therefore, no charges were made for any such actions committed by the Nazis that occurred before September of 1939, the beginning of WWII. (Schabas 2006)

At the first meeting of the General Assembly of the UN in 1946, the lesser states (which would be considered third world states), specifically Brazil, Cuba, India, and Panama, wishing to proactively rectify the possible lack of prosecution in the future, complained as to there being no mechanism to prevent or punish such crimes against humanity that occur in peace time. The result was UNGA Resolution 96i, defining genocide as a crime, as previously mentioned in this chapter. This resolution was to cover those particular crimes against humanity in times of peace, although the crime of genocide can be committed at any time and be prosecutable.

### *If it is not Genocide, what could it be?*

Believe it or not, not all inappropriate and misapplied accusations of genocide involve Israel. Indeed, while misapplying the term genocide is becoming more and more common, it has been misapplied ever since the designation of genocide, as punishable criminal behavior, and the convention defining it, went into effect. The UN Convention on the Prevention and Punishment of the Crime of Genocide was voted into being by the UN General Assembly on December 9, 1948. On January 12, 1951, the Genocide Convention went into force. In December of 1951, a petition was presented to the United Nations charging the United States with committing genocide against African Americans (Civil Rights Congress 1951, xi-xiii).

The petition itself was heart-rending. It truthfully listed the various crimes committed against African Americans, solely due to the color of their skin. Rank discrimination, as a cause of illiteracy, poverty, increased mortality, denial of justice, and denial of civil rights, as well as the blatant commission of crimes against humanity, directed toward African Americans, is well known and well proven. However, as evil a crime as it is, it did not come close to being genocide. Rather, it is almost identical to the South African system of Apartheid, with the exception that it was controlled by the states and not the US federal government, despite the institutionalized racism abundant within the federal government. It is clear that the discriminatory laws affecting the African American community in the American south were designed to maintain a status quo that saw African Americans as a source of inexpensive labor with no political rights, which was the same effect of Apartheid in South Africa. The same type behavior, as well as more subtle discriminatory law and behavior in the American north, was also a status quo issue but more socially than economically driven.

Therefore, as this repression and discrimination did not reflect the concept of the Genocide Convention, Lemkin himself opposed the petition. Samantha Powers, a noted genocide scholar and current US ambassador to the UN, observed that Lemkin believed that criminal discrimination and repression, without the intent to destroy a people, was covered under the UN's Universal Declaration of Human Rights. Lemkin, perhaps out of "ownership" issues, did not want the line between the two conventions blurred. Regardless, not only did Lemkin see this petition as an attack on his new homeland, it was also one that might make it appear that the Soviet Union, who supported the petition, had a higher moral position, thus diminishing the indignation arising from the genocidal crimes being committed by the Soviets against the Estonians, Latvians, Lithuanians, and Poles.

Adam Jones, in his discussion pertaining to the labeling of slavery of a specific people to be a case of genocide, considers such labeling as a "tendency to 'banalize' the genocide framework. Indeed, the purpose of slavery is the exploitation of labor, not the extinction of the laborer" (Jones 2006, 23-24).

There are several serious crimes that can occur when there is a conflict, whether or not a full scale war is ongoing, that while devastating, do not rise to the level of genocide. Some of these were not considered crimes at all during the time frame that they were committed. It could be said that the Palestinian Civil War that started in 1947 is still ongoing. After all, the Palestinians never surrendered or quit and they never signed a peace treaty, they just lost. Therefore, there is a possibility what is being decried as genocide are actually war crimes.

### What is a War Crime?
The international Criminal Court defines a war crime as:

> [A] grave breach of the Geneva Conventions and other serious violations of the laws and customs applicable in international armed conflict and in conflicts "not of an international character" listed in the Rome Statute, when they are committed as part of a plan or policy or on a large

scale. These prohibited acts include: murder; mutilation, cruel treatment and torture; taking of hostages; intentionally directing attacks against the civilian population; intentionally directing attacks against buildings dedicated to religion, education, art, science or charitable purposes, historical monuments or hospitals; pillaging; rape, sexual slavery, forced pregnancy or any other form of sexual violence; conscripting or enlisting children under the age of 15 years into armed forces or groups or using them to participate actively in hostilities. (ICC-CPI 2015)

Nowhere on this list is there ethnic cleansing, collateral damage including accidental attacks on buildings and/or civilians, building homes on occupied territory, allowing and even encouraging members of your own population to move into those homes.

The Laws of War, from which war crimes are naturally derived, have a long history. While the law's internationally recognized status starts from the 1850s, its foundation was likely laid well before the Peloponnesian Wars. Within Herodotus' histories, among other items, is a collection of the traditions regarding the conduct of states toward emissaries. The Yale Law School's Avalon Project contains the various treaties, conventions, conferences and agreements since the Declaration of Paris of 1856, the agreement concerning the conduct of warring parties with respect to neutral parties and their goods on the high seas. In essence, this compact was an agreement to end the practice of private navies (privateers) whose sole purpose was plunder at sea and could hardly be controlled by the sovereign power under which they were authorized. Interesting to note, this first agreement was made when it became possible to report the conduct of war on a daily basis due to the invention of the telegraph.

The Yale collection also has the Hague Conference of 1907 and all of the Geneva Conventions stretching from 1864 through 1975. It is the violation of these various laws that makes a crime a war crime. However, just with any code of law, the mere violation of a law does not indicate to what severity punishment should be meted. After all, it should not be a popularity contest wherein one is punished for a violation of a minor provision to the same extent one is punished for violation of a major provision just because the egregious party is out of favor with the international community.

While the major, or heinous, war crimes were listed on the previous page, there is a list of minor war crimes. This concept of "minor war crimes" derives from International Committee of the Red Cross' (ICRC) concept of war crimes. To that organization, war crimes have been committed even if the action was thwarted or perhaps never even occurred, thus the very act of aiming a cannon toward a civilian area is a war crime, even if a shot was never fired or the cannon was destroyed before it was ever loaded. Another general action, considered to be a war crime by the ICRC, is:

> Conduct (that) breaches important values. Acts may amount to war crimes because they breach important values, even without physically endangering persons or objects directly. These include, for example, abusing dead bodies; subjecting persons to humiliating treatment; making persons undertake work that directly helps the military operations of the enemy; (and) violation of the right to fair trial. (ICRC 2015)

Further, the ICRC uses an example from the International Criminal Tribunal for the former Yugoslavia as a reference as to what is a war crime, even though it is not a "serious" war crime (warranting prosecution):

> the appropriation of a loaf of bread belonging to a private individual by a combatant in occupied territory would violate Article 46(1) of the Hague Regulations, but would not amount to a "serious" violation of international humanitarian law. As seen from the examples of war crimes referred

to above, this does not mean that the breach has to re-sult in death or physical injury, or even the risk thereof, although breaches of rules protecting important values often result in distress and anxiety for the victims. (ICRC 2015)

Finally, the ICRC indicates that the crime does not even have to be a grave breach of a law of war to be prosecuted:

(The court) had to examine whether such violations entail individual criminal responsibility under customary interna-tional law or whether Additional Protocol I provides for indi-vidual criminal responsibility notwithstanding the fact that the violation is not listed as a grave breach. (ICRC 2015)

Incredulously, the ICRC also recognizes individual state statutes even though not seen in any treaty, convention, or agreement. "This practice does not exclude the possibility that a State may define under its nation-al law other violations of international humanitarian law as war crimes" (ICRC 2015). Therefore, any invented crime, committed during a time of war, for instance Jews praying on the Temple Mount during a war with Jordan, and Jordan wins, then Jordan can try those Jews for committing a war crime.

And there is more:

Earlier practice seems to indicate that a specific act did not necessarily have to be expressly recognized by the international community as a war crime for a court to find that it amounted to a war crime. This point is illustrated by many judgments by national courts which found the accused guilty of war crimes committed in the Second World War which were not listed in the Charters of the International Military Tribunals at Nuremberg and at Tokyo, such as the lack of fair trial, abuse of dead bodies, offending the religious sensibilities of prisoners of war, and misuse of the red cross emblem.

It appears that anything done that might upset anyone during a time of war can be declared a war crime. Coincidentally, Alex Margolin, an Israeli writer, suggests that the change in the way war is being conducted, mainly in the Middle East, but also elsewhere, might signal a need to change the rules of war.

### Why do we care what it is called?

Mahmood Mamdani, writing in the London Review of Books concerning the labeling of conflicts, such as those occurring in Darfur, Congo, and Iraq, discussed the meaning of numbers in a conflict. How can so many people be pushing to label the conflict in the Darfur region of Sudan, with a death toll in the hundreds of thousands, a genocide, while the death toll in Congo, with more than 4 million dead, is termed an insurgency? And why are the same people, who demand the United States end its intervention in Iraq, demanding intervention in Darfur, especially when the death toll and refugee numbers in both conflicts are at parity? A partial answer deals with the participants in each conflict. In Congo, it is an African against African conflict while Iraq is an Arab against Arab conflict. However, in Darfur, it is an Arab against African conflict.

Here Mamdani relies on Nicholas Kristof, a New York Times op-ed columnist who between 2004 and 2006 made six trips into Darfur to report on the conflict. He compares the death rate of the conflict with the annual death toll from Malaria, which is between one million and three million people a year. Kristoff explained that:

> We have a moral compass within us and its needle is moved not only by human suffering but also by human evil. That is what makes genocide special – not the number of deaths but the government policy behind them. And that

is why stopping genocide should be an even higher prior-
ity than saving lives from AIDS or malaria. (Mamdani 2007)

But Mamdani is not satisfied with this response. He believes there must
be more to this incongruity. He is right. As he opines later on – Genocide
is the reverse of the Nobel Prize. It is the sign you pin on the back of your
"worst enemy." The genocide label allows you to "vilify your adversaries
while ensuring impunity for your allies" (Mamdani 2007). This label is thus
attached to the enemy in the "war on terror." In the United States, this
enemy, regardless of whether it is right or wrong, has been generalized as
Arabs. Indeed, Gallop polls show during the conflict in Darfur time frame,
Iraq, Iran (not Arab but their proximity may give them status as "honorary"
Arabs in American eyes), and Syria garnered between 38% and 47% of
the vote as the perceived greatest enemies to America (Dvorsky 2014).

How does this affect the labeling of Israel? As the former consensus
"greatest threat to peace in the world" (The US has recently taken its
place), Israel is perceived by pro-Palestinian forces as their greatest enemy, even though far many more Palestinians have been killed by Arab
forces, and many have been forced to live in abysmal refugee camps for
decades by their Arab "hosts" (Fassed 2003). And what better way to en-
act pejorative judgment than to identify your enemy with a birth certificate
naming "genocidal warfare" as one of the parents?

# Chapter Three

# Inventing a Different Kind of Genocide

As previously discussed, the UN did not pursue the genocide convention to ensure that the atrocities committed by Nazi Germany during WWII, and the same committed by Turkey against the Armenians during WWI, would not be repeated, or if they were, suitably judged and punished. The war crimes committed by those two states were crimes that were already identified and covered under what passed for international law at that time. They are "crimes against humanity" and the German high command was charged under that section. However, those charges only covered such crimes as were committed during times of war. The charges did not cover the persecution of Jews, Roma, and other minority religious or national groups from 1933, when the Nazis ascended to the rule of Germany, through 1939, the official start of WW II, nor would they have covered the massacres against the Armenians in the 1890s (Schabas 2014).

The 1946 vote that established the crime of genocide came about so that there would be a statute under which to prosecute states that caused massive grievous harm to minorities within their own borders outside of war; harm to the extent that the scale of devastation is almost overwhelming (Schabas 2014). Of course, Israel has never committed such a crime, but that has not stopped anyone from making such claims. Because many reading of such a claim, that Israeli is committing genocide, believe the accusation is absurd, some accusers have started inventing terms in order to confuse the issue, yet still make it sound as if Israel is committing genocide.

John Docker is one such accuser that has published an essay claiming Israel is committing "memoricide," defined by Ilan Pappé as "erasure of the history of one people in order to write that of another people's over it" (Rashid 2014, 6). How one erases the history of a still existing subsector of the Arab people, a subsector that has grown from 1.3 million to over 12 million people in 70 years, is unfathomable. And if it were even possible, how is it a crime, other than as a crying shame?

During the October 2012 session of the Russell Tribunal on Palestine (Russell Tribunal), Israel was accused of committing sociocide (RToP 2012). While no official legal definition of this term (crime?) appears to exist, Daniel Machover, attorney and co-founder of Lawyers for Palestinian Human Rights and a functionary with the Russell Tribunal, provided a working definition to the Russell Tribunal:

> 'Sociocide' means ... a widespread or systematic attack directed against a population of people living in non-self-governing territory or a territory under foreign military occupation, with intent to prevent the people from exercising their collective right to self-determination. (Machover 2015)

Johan Galtung, a professor of peace studies and coiner of the word "sociocide" (along with ecocide and omnicide), testifying before the Russell Tribunal, defined sociocide as "the killing of a society's capacity to survive and to reproduce itself," and "the intended wounding-killing of a society by eliminating the prerequisites for a live, vibrant, dynamic society" (Galtung 2012). Amazingly, the two definitions appear to have nothing to do with each other even though there is sure to be a convoluted path invented one day to join them together.

Of course, this tribunal certainly had its own controversy and dysfunctions with definitions, as reported by Abraham Greenhouse:

> The most frustrating moment for myself personally, as an activist, was the Tribunal's hours-long deliberation over terminology, particularly the question of whether

Israel's policies on Palestinians would be better characterized by the terms "genocide" or "sociocide" (the latter
of which has no formal legal definition). While there were
important legal arguments being made about the impli-
cations of the use of one term over another, the descent
into such bickering over semantics (to the point of lawyer
Michael Mansfield actually yelling at Palestinian political
scientist Saleh Abdeljawad) made this diplomacy-based
discourse seem all the more diversionary and irrelevant.
(Greenhouse 2012)

It is interesting to note that Keith Doubt considers the ethnic cleansing
of Bosnia to be case of sociocide rather than genocide (Doubt 2006,
126). Of course, Doubt also states that sociocide cannot succeed
(Doubt 2006, 22). Hanan Chehata, a. prolific writer for the Middle East
Monitor and the holder of a Ph.D. in Law, relates that "Global leaders
and, indeed, the population of the world at large are increasingly view-
ing Israel's treatment of the Palestinian people as an unmitigated form of
genocide" (Chehata 2010, 4). Of course, no citation follows this charge.
Not surprisingly as there does not appear to be a poll performed that
substantiates such an accusation. Finally,. Chehata accuses Israel of
committing "Cultural" genocide against the Palestinians. Of course,
like most non-historians, Chehata incorrectly infers the reason for the
genocide convention as a remedy and a means of punishment for any
duplication of criminal activity as in Nazi Germany's genocidal rampage
throughout Europe.

For this type genocide, Chehata relies on Nersessian's definition:

"Cultural genocide extends beyond attacks upon the
physical and/or biological elements of a group and seeks
to eliminate its wider institutions. This is done in a variety of ways, and often includes the abolition of a group's
language, restrictions upon its traditional practices and

ways, the destruction of religious institutions and objects, the persecution of clergy members, and attacks on academics and intellectuals. Elements of cultural genocide are manifested when artistic, literary, and cultural activities are restricted or outlawed and when national treasures, libraries, archives, museums, artifacts, and art galleries are destroyed or confiscated." (Chehata 2010, 4)

Further cheapening the meaning of genocide, Chehata asserts that the cultural variety "can be as equally devastating in its impacts as genocide itself." In her attempt to offer evidence of a so called cultural genocide, Chehata goes through a litany of canards as proof. "It is widely acknowledged that although most of the world accepts and recognizes the modern state of Israel, for many countries, there is no such place as Palestine" (Chehata 2010, 6). A strange notion as Arafat's initial declaration of Palestinian independence in 1988 is recognized by approximately 130 states. In contrast, Israel has been a member state of the United Nations for over 65 years yet only 160 states out of 192 recognize it.

Lemkin did have the notion that genocide had a cultural aspect. Indeed, he desired that the Genocide Convention include it in the definitions. However, Lemkin did not consider enforced assimilation as genocide.

"Terms like "denationalization" or "Germanization" of foreign peoples were not synonyms with genocide, he thought, because "they treat mainly the cultural, economic, and social aspects of genocide, leaving out the biological aspects, such as causing the physical decline and even destruction of the population involved." In Lemkin's notion of ethnogenesis, the "biological and physical structure" was elemental, so that policies that attack a group's culture—its morality, for instance—are only genocidal when motivated by the intention to destroy this structure. His unpublished manuscripts confirm this interpretation. The gradual assimilation of a people by processes of "cultural diffusion," even that entailing the incremental disintegration of a culture, was not genocidal… (D. Moses 2004, 23)

Another canard is that the denial of the fictitious Palestinian "right of return" "is one of the most obvious ways in which Israel is attempting to destroy their culture" (Chehata 2010, 6). Of course, that is easily disputed by the Armenians who, despite undergoing genocide wherein they lost over 1.5 million men, women, and children, and despite that they were exiled from their home of 3000 years, Anatolia, over 100 years ago, have maintained their rich culture in other lands. The same can be said of the Jews who also maintained a rich cultural life, despite their various exiles and having undergone several episodes of genocidal violence, such as the Spanish Inquisition, the Russian and Polish pogroms, and one of the most horrific genocides in history, the Holocaust. But the claim that the Palestinians, who have grown from 1.3 million in 1948 to over 12 million today, are in danger of losing their culture, is surely a joke.

Chehata insists that the removal of the term "West Bank" from Israeli maps, following the 1967 war, replaced with its original names, Judea and Samaria, is a denial of Palestinian presence (Chehata 2010, 6). However, she fails to mention that the term "West Bank" has only been in use since 1950, having its origination only 17 years before the Six Day War and coined by Jordan when it had annexed the area to differentiate it from Jordan's "East Bank." This renaming and annexing of Judea and Samaria was a signal that no Palestinian state would ever come into being (Tessler 2009, 276). Before then, as mentioned in the 1947 UNGA partition resolution setting out the partition boundaries, the area was called "the hill country of Samaria and Judea" (UN 1947). Therefore, Israel merely returned the names to their official ones, just as they were known by 17 years earlier, with approximately the same people living there.

The next fable spun by Chehata deals with the supposed Israeli plan for the destruction of the Al-Aqsa Mosque situated on the Temple Mount. The Mosque, the third holiest site for Muslims, sitting on the holiest site for Jews, the Temple Mount, has been a source of contention for years. However, Chehata claims that when Palestine was "under Muslim leadership, all were free to worship in their own ways." Of course, there is no citation for that bit of nonsense as, ostensibly, worship at the wall was the pretext for the Arab riots of 1929 that resulted in the murder of many religious Jews (Hollander 2009), and the area was forbidden to Jews by the Jordanians during the 19 years (1949-1967) they occupied Jerusalem (Camera 2007a).

After Israel captured and annexed Jerusalem in 1967, the holy sites were open to all but with the understanding that Jews would not worship on the Temple Mount. Additionally, in a conciliatory diplomatic move, Israel "immediately ceded internal administrative control of the Temple Mount compound to the Jordanian Waqf (Islamic trust) while overall security control of the area was maintained by Israel" (Camera 2007b).

Chehata claims that Israelis have been excavating under Al-Aqsa Mosque in order to cause a collapse or such unsafe conditions as to tear it down. However, the truth is that Palestinians have been doing the excavations to enlarge the worship areas under the mosque. Chehata's source is a pamphlet published by "Friends of Al-Aqsa Organization" (Chehata 2010, 21). Among her many other exaggerations is: "Israeli forces caused significant damage to the Commonwealth war cemetery in Gaza" wherein all of six grave stones, out of thousands, and a wall was damaged (Chehata 2010, 14). After all of this, it is not unkind to seriously consider the possibility that Chehata does not have a doctorate. After all, her biography lacks any information on where she obtained any of her degrees.

In her conclusion, Chehata states that "prominent Israeli figures have admitted that several forms of genocide are taking place" (Chehata 2010, 19) Forgetting for the moment that there is only one form of genocide, as proof, she cites Professor Lev Ginsberg's 2004 article in which he accuses Israel of committing "Symbolic Genocide." Ginsberg's definition of this type of genocide, with its prologue, is as follows:

> "Every people has its symbols, national leaders and political institutions, a home land, past and future generations, and hopes. All these symbolically represent a people. Israel is systematically damaging, destroying and eradicating all of these, with unbelievable bureaucratic jargon." (Chehata 2010, 19)

With this, Grinberg claims that "(t)he government of Israel is turning the Palestinians into a nation of Shahids (martyrs), and the Middle Eastern conflict into a holy war-jihad-crusade." But Ginsberg appears to avoid the fact that Arab leaders declared the conflict to be a holy war-jihad (they would not use the word "crusade" to describe their actions) back in 1948 (Morris 2010). Additionally, Ginsberg claims that Israel's actions are an "existential threat to the Palestinian people" (Grinberg 2004), a people who have managed through unbearable hardship to slightly increase their number from 1.3 million to about 12 million in 67 years while the Jewish people are just now approaching pre-holocaust population figures (MEMO 2014).

As for events that might actually be described as some sort of cultural genocide, consider the current activity by the "Islamic State in the Levant" (ISIL) wherein they have destroyed countless cultural heritage buildings and statues in the name of Islamization. Another example is the Bosnian Serbs who destroyed the Bosnian National Library during the ethnic cleansing of Bosniaks in the 1990s. The Taliban destruction of the Buddhas of Bamiyan in 2001 is obviously meant to destroy any part of Afghan culture that is not Islamic. Lemkin singled out an example of "the attempt to destroy the cultural fabric and continuity of particular groups" – the Nazi destruction of Lublin's Talmudic Library (Cox 2011, 6). On the other hand, the Jews recued the books of the Palestinians so that they would not be wantonly destroyed by looters, acts of war, or the ravages of the environment as abandoned property. While noted in a pejorative manner by the Institute for Palestinian Studies (Amit 2010), the very fact that the 30,000 volumes collected are housed and available in the Jewish National and University Library, rather than destroyed, speaks to the lack of intent to obliterate what is considered Palestinian culture through the destruction of their books.

### Colonial Enterprise as Inherently Genocidal

Dirk Moses, Professor of Global and Colonial History at the European University Institute, writes extensively on genocide as a result of colonial activity. He ponders the hypocrisy of Britain and France as champions of humanitarian intervention while being the "world's prime imperialists and founders of settler colonies that dispossessed and often extermi-nated Indigenous peoples" (D. Moses 2013, 37). In doing so, he considers whether or not colonialism is inherently genocidal.

Docker follows Moses with his own question, not if colonialism is genocidal, but whether it is inherent or constitutive (Docker 2010). *Open Democracy* takes the accusation one step further when charges Israel with being a white supremacist settler colonial state in the same man-ner as French Algeria and Dutch South Africa, worthy of all of the liberal world's condemnation (Open Democracy 2015).

Again, a standard antisemitic/anti-Zionist canard comes out; "After some debate amongst the Zionist leadership, Palestine was nominated as the Jewish 'homeland.'" The truth of the matter is that attainment of the Jewish homeland in Palestine proved to be extremely difficult, as it was under the control of the Ottoman Empire, so temporary refuges were proposed as the need for such was great. However, each proposal was overwhelmingly voted down as the original Jewish homeland was in the Palestinian region and recreation of that homeland was the goal of the majority of delegates to the Zionist Congresses.

British control of Palestine was important to Britain because it was a backdoor to the Suez Canal and a shorter passage to India, but in no way was it a British colony and in no way did it enrich Britain. In fact, it was a financial drain. Additionally, Palestine was not a Jewish colony in that all

Jewish funds invested helped the growth of Palestine. No funds went out of Palestine to enrich a Jewish state elsewhere, as there was no Jewish state elsewhere.

So whether or not a colonial enterprise is inherently genocidal is a moot point as Israel was never a colonial enterprise. It was always the restoration of the Jewish state by the descendants of the people of the Jewish kingdoms in the region.

# Chapter Four

# The 2013 Kuala Lumpur War Crimes Tribunal

The Kuala Lumpur War Crimes Commission (KLWCC), also known as the Kuala Lumpur War Crimes Tribunal (KLWCT), is an unofficial Malaysian organization established in 2007 by senior Malaysian statesman, Dr. Mahathir Mohamad. Mohamad, Prime Minister of Malaysia from 1981 to 2003, purportedly set up the Commission as an alternative forum to the International Criminal Court (ICC). It appears Mohamad's major complaint was that the ICC was only prosecuting crimes committed in Africa, by black Africans, and deliberately failing to note the seriousness of crimes committed in the Middle East, allegedly by Israel, or on the behalf of Israel.

The KLWCT's first court case in 2011 ended with the conviction, in *abstentia*, of former US President George W. Bush and former British Prime Minister Tony Blair for "crimes against peace," stemming from the 2003 invasion of Iraq. The second case, in 2012, also involved trying and convicting Bush, again in *abstentia,* as well as several prominent American ex-officials for war crimes, specifically for the torture of prisoners in Iraq and Afghanistan. The third case, held in 2013, involved trying Israel and an Israeli general, Amos Yaron, for war crimes, for crimes against humanity, and for committing genocide. The charges against General Yaron were as follows:

> "The Defendant Amos Yaron perpetrated War Crimes, Crimes Against Humanity, and Genocide in his capacity as the Commanding Israeli General in military control of

the Sabra and Shatila refugee camps in Israeli occupied Lebanon in September of 1982 when he knowingly facilitated and permitted the large-scale Massacre of the residents of those two camps in violation of the Hague Regulations on Land Warfare of 1907; the Fourth Geneva Convention of 1949; the 1948 Genocide Convention; the Nuremberg Charter (1945), the Nuremberg Judgment (1946), and the Nuremberg Principles (1950); customary international law, *jus cogens*, the Laws of War, and International Humanitarian Law." (KLWCT 2013)

The charges against Israel were as follows:

"From 1948 and continuing to date the State of Israel (hereafter 'the Defendant') carried out against the Palestinian people a series of acts namely killing, causing serious bodily harm and deliberately inflicting conditions of life calculated to bring about physical destruction.

The conduct of the Defendant was carried out with the intention of destroying in whole or in part the Palestinian people.

These acts were carried out as part of a manifest pattern of similar conduct against the Palestinian people.

These acts were carried out by the Defendant through the instrumentality of its representatives and agents including those listed in Appendices 1 and 2.

Such conduct constitutes the Crime of Genocide under international law including the Convention on the Prevention and Punishment of Genocide 1948 ('the Genocide Convention') in particular Article II and punishable under Article III of the said Convention. It also constitutes the crime of genocide as stipulated in Article 10 of the Charter of the Kuala Lumpur Foundation to Criminalise (sic) War.

> Such conduct by the Defendant as an occupying pow-
> er also violates customary international law as embodied
> in the Hague Convention of 1907 Respecting the Laws
> and Customs of War on Land, and the Fourth Geneva
> Convention of 1949.
> Such conduct also constitutes War Crimes and Crimes
> against Humanity under international law. (KLWCT 2013)

This third trial was held in Kuala Lumpur, Malaysia, beginning in November of 2012 with a preliminary enquiry and with the trial itself starting 21 August 2013, scheduled to finish on the 24th. However, nothing went as planned. On the 21st, with seven judges sitting on the bench, the prosecuting attorneys, led by Professor Gurdial Singh Nijar, without previous disclosure, proceeded to argue for the recusal of one of the judges, Judge Eric David.

Eric David, a Professor and the President of the Centre of International Law at the Free University of Brussels, and President of the Advisory Commission on International Humanitarian Law of the Belgian Red Cross, was accused by the co-prosecutor, Francis A. Boyle, in some convoluted way, of being a supporter of Mossad, the Israeli Secret Service. Boyle's accusation stems from a rendered judgment, by David, that an Iranian political group, the People's Mujahedeen Organization of Iran (PMOI), is not a terrorist organization. Boyle claimed the PMOI is; linked with Mossad, dedicated to regime change in Iran, and thus David could not possibly be an unbiased judge in a trial wherin the charge of genocide is filed against Israel. As Boyle provided no evidence other than an undated photocopy of David's legal opinion regarding the PMOI, and another photocopy of a newspaper article about the judgment, unsurprisingly, the court ruled against Boyle.

With this ruling, the prosecutorial team announce that the witnesses refused to testify in front of Judge David as they feared for their safety once they returned home. Again, no evidence was presented of any reason for such fear. Regardless, the court was forced to adjourn for the day. The second day, the prosecutor stated that the witnesses again refused to testify with Judge David on the bench. One of the witnesses addressed the court, stating the same fears, but producing no evidence as to these fears being justified. The prosecutor then requested that the proceeding by adjourned indefinitely.

The court's statements, prior to ruling on the request for adjournment, reflected on the contempt of the prosecutorial team for the Tribunal's rulings. They also reflected on the lack of any evidence to support the fears of the witnesses, the waste of funds and time provided to afford the witnesses "their day in court," and that the trial had ground to a deadlock because of the prosecution's unreasonable demands, even though the prosecution previously swore to abide by the Tribunal's rulings. Finally, the court stated that the prosecution's actions were intolerable and could not be condoned by the Tribunal. The court then adjourned indefinitely.

This was not Boyle's only act of misconduct during this particular episode. Boyle investigated the background of another judge, although the results of that examination were not brought up in the courtroom. It appears that Judge Michael Hourigan, a human rights attorney, had served the United Nations, the FBI, the CIA, and Scotland Yard. Boyle, in several interviews, "suggested that these organizations were the very ones that were connected to the atrocities perpetuated by the Israeli forces in Palestine, and having Judge Hourigan on the bench would compromise the fairness and impartiality of the Tribunal" (Carrim n.d.).

The Tribunal reopened in November 0f 2013. The new members of the court were Dr. Mahathir Mohamad (Chairman), Prof. Michel Chossudovsky, Dr. Denis Halliday, Mr. Musa Ismail, Dr. Zulaiha Ismail, Dr. Yaacob Merican, and Dr. Hans von Sponeck. Unsurprisingly, Francis Boyle was nowhere to be seen. Perhaps with the founder of the Tribunal acting as chair, there was confidence that the previous shenanigans which had forced the court to adjourn earlier would not be a factor. On a humorous aside, it appears that certain parties believe that Boyle deliberately attempted to start an:

> (I)nternecine war upon targeted Judges of the Kuala Lumpur War Crimes Tribunal, and thereby destabilize the Tribunal. That internecine war, induced by a standard

covert operating Cointelpro procedures of U.S., U.K. and Israeli intelligence agencies known as "Meme warfare", had the specific objectives of (1) destabilizing the Tribunal by making it a "shooting gallery for shooting down or disqualifying Judges" so that multiple Judges could be disqualified as "Zionists" on specious grounds; (2) discrediting the Tribunal as an objective adjudicatory body in the area of war crimes; (3) discrediting it as a functioning body to deliver credible justice in the area of Israel war crimes in Palestine 1948 – Present. (Webre 2013)

Regardless, the limitations of the Tribunal remained.

The authority of this Tribunal, as reported in The Diplomat, is nonexistent (Diplomat 2012). Additionally, the sole punishment able to be exercised by the court seems to be that "the name of the guilty person will be entered in the Commission's Register of War Criminals and publicized worldwide." Therefore, Israel (and likely the rest of the Western World) ignored the summons, the proceedings, and the ruling. As a sign of their indifference, Israel sent no representation and no witnesses.

Noting this predictable behavior (it does not appear that any defendant has ever appeared before this tribunal), the court appointed an *Amicus Curiae* team to stand for the defense of Israel and General Yaron, at least pertaining to matters of the court and the prosecution following the law. This team did challenge the rules in accordance with standard criminal law but was curiously overridden by the court, inadvertently proving its illegitimacy. The Tribunal prosecutor put forth that there could be no violation of criminal court procedures in that the Tribunal "is governed by its own rules..."

The trail proceeded in an orderly manner with only prosecutorial witnesses as there were no witnesses for the defense. Regarding the charges against General Yaron related to genocide committed in the refugee camps of Sabra and Shatila, a witness claimed that 3500 people had been killed and that it was the Phalangists (Lebanese Arab fighters allied with Israel), who did the actual killing, and that they were working with the Israelis. The defense attorneys did not question any facts or allegations. The second witness claimed that 1350 Palestinians were killed. Again, the defense remained silent, never questioning the contradictory testimonies. The third witness testified that British National Archives stated that 3500 people had died in the camps. A copy of this document was not produced in court. In fact, the British National Archives state *that as many as* 3500 may have been killed; quite a different fact. Indeed, several reports regarding the death toll from the two refugee camps have been written, promoting figures of anywhere from 762 up to 3500 (Reese 2013).

It does not appear that the defense challenged the 3500 figure, despite the lack of evidence of any figure being a true number of casualties. Additionally, one expert witness, Bayan Nuwayhed al-Hout, testified that she was unable to get a list of the names of the victims although she had contacted several international organizations to get such a list.

The 8th witness was Ilan Pappé, a "new historian," whose testimony dealt with, in his opinion, the 1948 expulsion of 700,000 Palestinians from the territory that became Israel being an act of genocide deliberately committed by the State of Israel. Additionally, Pappé's testimony covered other historical data. Keeping in mind that Pappé is a trained historian with a doctorate in the field, some of his inaccuracies are troubling. Pappé testified that most of the Jews in British Mandate Palestine arrived three years before Israel's independence. However, data supplied by Esco Foundation, the actual 1941 population figures published in 1947 show a Jewish population of 474,000 and the 1945 population figure estimate of 608,000 along with the Israeli estimate of 650,000 in 1947 and the 1937 estimate of 386,000 clearly shows the bulk of the Jewish population arrived at least ten years before independence (ESCO 2010).

Pappé also testified that the UN delegation that developed the partition plan that was accepted in 1947 also had a minority plan. Pappé claims that this minority plan, which called for an overall Palestinian population vote as to what path to follow regarding the dissolution of British

Mandate Palestine, had the same support as the accepted plan, among the UN membership. However, there is no record stating that the minority plan had this level of support nor did Pappé provide any proof of such support.

Additionally, Pappé testified regarding Israeli deputy defense minister Matan Vilnai's statement, that the Palestinians would bring on a "bigger 'shoah' upon themselves," stating that such a declaration could only be seen as a threat of genocide in that the word shoah has no other meaning in Hebrew other than the extermination of the Jews by Nazi Germany during WWII. However, Ha'aretz appears to disagree. They reported:

> Deputy Defense Minister Matan Vilnai went as far as threatening a "shoah," the Hebrew word for holocaust or disaster. The word is generally used to refer to the Nazi Holocaust, but a spokesman for Vilnai said the deputy defense minister used the word in the sense of "disaster," saying "he did not mean to make any allusion to the genocide." (Ha'aretz 2008)

Ha'aretz, the liberal Israeli newspaper of record, is not considered to be friendly to any conservative Israeli government or politician. So if Ha'aretz states that the word "shoah" has more than one meaning, Pappé is likely wrong.

Pappé's testimony continued with reference to a group of anonymous soldiers reporting alleged atrocities committed during times of war in Gaza as being "brave." As it takes no act of bravery to accuse someone of a crime when your identity is hidden, it is ridiculous to characterize such testimony as brave and an objective person cannot take such testimony seriously.

Finally, Pappé's statement, echoed by many, that Gaza is the most densely populated area in the world, is absurd. Gaza's population density isn't even close to the top 50 cities in the world nor, on a state wide basis, even a quarter of Macau's density.

This final exaggeration shows that Pappé is not so much a historian as he is, as describe by Benny Morris, also an Israeli "new historian," "one of the world's sloppiest historians; at worst, one of the most dishonest. In truth, he probably merits a place somewhere between the two" (Morris 2011). More to the point might be Leslie Stein's condemnation: "Ilan Pappé is far less interested in the veracity of his sources and is far more concerned to denigrate the entire Zionist enterprise..." (Stein 2011, 129)

None of Pappé's testimony was challenged by the assigned, and what now could be pejoratively and derisively described as the "alleged," defense team. This despite the fact that not only is all of the information provided by Pappé available online, all of the scholarly refutation of that same information is available online. Like the disreputable historian of the German side of WW II, David Irving, Pappé's writing is bent with a political aspect in that interpretation is made to reflect Pappé's political opinion and not what the actual facts portray.

While referring to a different set of defendants in another KLWCT trial, *The Diplomat* offered this scathing critique of the KLWCT;

> Mahathir's antics and the unconventional tactics of the KLWCT simply detract from tribunals where very serious issues are being dealt with, such as the genocides in Cambodia and Rwanda. Despite their flaws (and there are many) they hold a recognition backed by a U.N. mandate that legitimizes their investigations, prosecutions and findings among the public and victims they serve.
>
> The Kuala Lumpur tribunal holds none of these characteristics. Mahathir is an old political stager and may have had his day in court, which should delight him. But to be clear in regards to... the War on Terror, no one else has legitimately had theirs. (Diplomat 2012)

# Chapter Five

# Palestine in an International Historical Perspective on Genocide

Martin Shaw, a sociology Ph.D. and genocide theorist teaching at the University of Sussex (notorious for its cancelled conference on whether or not Israel has the right to exist (Firsht 2015)), produced the paper that is the basis for this chapter's heading (Shaw 2010), which was later revisited by Shaw in 2013. The paper suggests that the exodus of 80% of the Arab population, from what became Israel, should be treated as a case of genocide.

This movement of approximately 750,000 people during a civil war that morphed into a regional war, had a loss of life of a few thousand (Shaw 2010, 18), with most scholars suggesting between 5,000 (Shaw 2013, 6) and 6,000 (Masalha 2003). Many anti-Israel writers and scholars do not mention a number, preferring to dwell on the individual massacres, perhaps in an effort to make them seem more horrific than the numbers actually portray. The Arab exodus, from that part of British Mandate Palestine that became Israel, was due to several factors. There is the usual movement of the wealthy and the political elites during times of trouble, a large portion of the rest of the population having a fear of harm, exacerbated by both the Jewish and Arab propaganda about the massacre at Deir Yassin (Masalha 2003, 32-33), and actually being forced out by Jewish armed forces. While every loss of innocent life is a tragedy, the lack of significant casualties among the Arabs, when compared to similar episodes of mass population movement during times of conflict, can only be explained by the policies of the Jewish/Israeli provisional government and the conduct of the provisional armed forces (Lozowick 2003, 99-100). This is in marked contrast between the forced population movements during the India/Pakistan partition in 1947 wherein millions died (Dalrymple 2015), the expulsion of ethnic Germans from Poland and Czechoslovakia after WW II wherein two million, and possibly seven million, died (Kurth 1990, 376), and the Turkish/Greek population exchange during the 1920s wherein approximately one million Greeks were killed and one million Greeks fled in terror prior to the exchange (Tsilfidis 2015).

It should be noted that one of the prosecuting attorneys at the KLWCT, Francis A. Boyle, sought to prove Israel had committed genocide by analogizing the decision of the World Court regarding the order issued to Yugoslavia to cease committing all acts of genocide, in that the death count from the Bosnia conflict, 10 percent of the Muslim population (250,000), as well as the murder, execution style, of almost 8,000 Bosniaks in Srebrenica (over a three day period of time), showed "intent to destroy in substantial part the national, ethnical, racial, and different religious group (Jews versus Muslims and Christians) constituting the Palestinian people" (Boyle 2013b). In this manner, Boyle attempts to show that even the loss of 5,000 Palestinians over a 14-month period of time, out of a population of 1.2 million, should be considered genocide.

Of course, Boyle fails to note that the loss of 10 percent of the Palestinians who were in the portion of British Mandate Palestine that became Israel would have meant 90,000 fatalities if a true comparison to Bosnia were to be made. If only counting 10 percent of those that fled that same territory, there would have been 75,000 fatalities. However, as stated earlier, the total fatalities were between 5,000 and 6,000, less than 1 percent of those that fled and less than a half pecent of the total population. Further, the time frame for that loss of life was over 14 months, as compared to the three days of the Srebrenica massacre, with a death toll 20 to 40 percent higher. Finally, Boyle never tells the court that the International Court of Justice (ICJ), in 2007 (six years before Boyle's declaration), ruled that Yugoslavia (Serbia) did not commit genocide in Bosnia (ICJ 2007)

Shaw cautions against equating the non-totality of Arab removal as being proof of a lack of genocidal intent in that neither Bosnia not Darfur experienced total population removal. However, Shaw fails to relate that the failure of the Serbs and the Sudanese to complete their goals was only through a lack of ability, not a lack of intent, especially as the charge of genocide can only be made if intent exists. Additionally, despite Shaw's opinion, the Tribunal trying Serbia did not find ethnic cleansing itself to be a case of genocide. In fact, the ICJ deliberately stated "(n)either the intent, as a matter of policy, to render an area ethnically homogeneous, nor the operations that may be carried out to implement such policy, can as such be designated as genocide" (ICJ 2007). In Israel's case, there is ample proof of a lack of intent as those who remained were deemed by the government to be non-threatening to the state, not that they were no longer identifiable as Arabs.

Regardless, trying to identifying any episode of Israel's conduct as genocidal requires changing the "sociological concept" of genocide as Shaw himself admits. Shaw states that this historical episode does not lend itself to a comparison with any other episode in history, based on scale, murderousness, ideological motivation, and any number of other comparatives (Shaw 2010, 2).

Shaw states that it is reasonable to bring up the possibility that the Palestinians underwent a genocide as a counter to Israel's frequent use of their own victimization, in that the Jews underwent such an episode wherein a third of all the Jews on Earth, during that time period, were murdered, during the Holocaust, to "validate its existence," and to validate the importance of a Jewish state existing as a permanent refuge. Unfortunately, Shaw fails to realize, or refuses to acknowledge, that while the Holocaust alone amply justifies the need for a Jewish controlled refuge for Jews world-wide, as the world did next to nothing to help rescue Jews from Nazi Germany's genocidal persecution, the number of pogroms and massacres and expulsions directed at Jews over the centuries adds exclamation points to that justification. Additionally, using Norman Finkelstein as the reference for Shaw's allegation is quite pejorative on its own, as the source is Finkelstein's book, "The Holocaust Industry" wherein Israel is accused of exploiting the Holocaust, and its victims, for its own, alleged, ill-gotten gain (Finkelstein 2000). Naturally, Finkelstein's book is widely discussed, and available for sale, in a variety of antisemitic, white supremacist, Holocaust denial, and radical Islamist websites such as David Irving's website, StormFront, IHR, and ElectronicIntifada, among others. University of Southampton Professor of Modern Jewish History, David Cesarani, describes Finkelstein's book as a "short, vitriolic polemic..." and that Finkelstein's "argument, flimsy as it is, rests on the misinterpretation of history and questionable use of sources" (Cesarani 2000). Along this same line, Shaw asserts that a Palestinian claim of genocide would cancel the same claim in Israel's, in his suitable for framing statement, foundational "myths"; another pejorative term, regardless of his parenthesized disclaimer about the use of "myth"(Shaw 2010, 2).

One of Shaw's major points, regarding his discussion of the definition of genocide, appears to revolve around the need to change the general understanding of what is legally genocide, to a general definition of genocide, which in Shaw's words, is more in tune with Lemkin's thoughts. In turn, this would likely expand the number of events, designated as genocidal, which have occurred. So much so that every century since the dawn of mankind can be called a "century of genocide." But Lemkin did not believe this maxim, that genocide is a common occurrence in modern history. He believed that such occurrences were rare since the Reformation. Again, Lemkin, when referring to Hitler's speech regarding the victor's right to "destroy tribes, entire people," stated that "the crime of the Reich in wantonly and deliberately wiping out whole peoples is not utterly new in the world. It is only new to the civilized world as we have come to think of it" (Frey 2009, 3).

Regardless, Shaw appears to channel his own "personal" Lemkin so that he can utilize his own personal definition of genocide as the final arbiter of the notion. Shaw believes that Lemkin considered expulsion to be a form of genocide. In this, he decries the Genocide Convention's deliberate exclusion of expulsion as a form of genocide in his belief that such is "the most common method through which states (and others) deliberately destroyed national, ethnic and other groups" (Shaw 2010, 16). Again, Shaw's inappropriate use of the word "destroy" is intended to invoke the Genocide Convention and it does not take a strong imagination to conclude that this new definition would likely include every violent event committed by Israel during the 1947-49 Israeli-Arab war.

Additionally, by linking his "new" definition to the UN Convention, Shaw might believe that he brings a counter to the frequent, in Shaw's terms, Israeli "claim" of the genocidal intent of its enemies. Of course, the use of the word "claim" rather than the more accurate "reporting" is another pejorative term employed by Shaw. After all, can the retelling of the threats, both in print and oral transmission, coming from Arab and other Muslim leadership over the last 70 years, be considered just a claim? Here are just a few examples of these threats:

> An October 11, 1947 report on the pan-Arab summit in the Lebanese town of Aley, by *Akhbar al-Yom*'s editor Mustafa Amin, contained an interview he held with Arab League secretary-general Azzam. Titled, "A War of Extermination," the interview read as follows (translated by Efriam Karsh: Abdul Rahman Azzam Pasha spoke to me about the horrific war that was in the offing... saying: "I personally wish that the Jews do not drive us to this war, as this will be a war of extermination and momentous massacre which will be spoken of like the Tartar massacre or the Crusader wars." (Barnett 2011)
>
> In March 1948, Haj Amin al-Husseini informed an interviewer in a Jaffa newspaper, *Al Sarah,* that the Arabs "would continue fighting until the Zionists were annihilated and the whole of Palestine became a purely Arab state."' Such genocidal intentions were imbibed by Arab fighters in the field. Al-Hassan Kam al-Màz, Safed's Arab section's military commander, in a cable to Arab Liberation

Army regional headquarters, assured his superiors that "morale is very strong, the young are enthusiastic, we will slaughter them [the Jews]." (Stein 2011, 139)

The national aim: the eradication of Israel." – President Nasser of Egypt, November 18, 1965, "Our basic objective will be the destruction of Israel – Nasser, May 27, 1967. (Camera 2007c) Cairo Radio statements: May 19, 1967: "This is our chance, Arabs, to deal Israel a mortal blow of annihilation, to blot out its entire presence in our holy land" (Camera 2007c). May 22, 1967: "The Arab people is firmly resolved to wipe Israel off the map" (Camera 2007c). May 30, 1967: "With the closing of the Gulf of Akaba, Israel is faced with two alternatives either of which will destroy it; it will either be strangled to death by the Arab military and economic boycott, or it will perish by the fire of the Arab forces encompassing it from the South, from the North, and from the East" (Camera 2007c).

From Iraq: "The existence of Israel is an error which must be rectified. This is our opportunity to wipe out the ignominy which has been with us since 1948. Our goal is clear – to wipe Israel off the map. We shall, God willing, meet in Tel Aviv and Haifa." – President Abdel Rahman Aref of Iraq, May 31, 1967 (Camera 2007c).

From the Palestinians: "We shall destroy Israel and its inhabitants and as for the survivors – if there are any – the boats are ready to deport them." – Shukairy, June 1, 1967, speaking at a Friday sermon in Jerusalem (Camera 2007c).

From Syria: Syria's forces are "ready not only to repulse the aggression, but to initiate the act of liberation itself, and to explode the Zionist presence in the Arab homeland. The Syrian army, with its finger on the trigger, is united…. I, as a military man, believe that the time has come to enter into a battle of annihilation." – Syrian Defense Minister (later Prime Minister and President) Hafez Assad, May 20, 1967 (Camera 2007c).

"I swear to God that if Israel dares to hit even one piece of steel on any industrial site, we will make the fire eat half of Israel," Saddam Hussein warned in a mid-afternoon address broadcast over state radio (Williams

1990). BBC News report in 2000: Iraqi leader Saddam Hussein has said his country could destroy Israel if it was given access to land next to the Jewish state (Gardener 2000).

Of course, there is all of the genocidal rhetoric from Iran regarding wiping Israel of the map, removing the Zionist regime, removing Israel from the pages of history, and the other various threats including the infamous statement:

> "If one day, the Islamic world is also equipped with weapons like those that Israel possesses now, then the imperialists' strategy will reach a standstill because the use of even one nuclear bomb inside Israel will destroy everything. However, it will only harm the Islamic world. It is not irrational to contemplate such an eventuality." Former Iranian President Ali Akbar Hashemi Rafsanjani Dec. 14, 2001. (Goldhagen 2009, 503)

Shaw's retort is his own list of one Israeli supposedly calling for genocide of the Palestinians, notably a deputy defense minister's (Matan Vilnai, noted previously in Ilan Pappé's testimony) statement that the Palestinians would bring on a "bigger shoah" upon themselves. Other than by semi-fanatical Israel bashers, Vilnai's comment rarely comes up, and as the issuer was only a deputy minister, he is hardly one who makes official government policy.

Shaw's next major point deals with what he considers the destruction of Arab society in British Mandate Palestine. In that his definition of the genocidal act states destruction, it seems that rather than using typical terminology such as "elimination," "removal," or "dismantling," Shaw uses a term associated with genocide, no matter how inappropriate. Of course, the Palestinian political leadership, along with some of that society, was "destroyed" during the 1936-1939 Arab Revolt. Further, the man who would nominally be considered the head of Arab society in British Mandate Palestine, Mohammed Effendi Amin el-Husseini, Grand Mufti of Jerusalem and President of the Supreme Muslim Council, was absent from the region throughout WW II.

As for the 1947-1949 time-frame, there cannot be much of a society when the entire region becomes a battleground. Regardless, it does not matter what Shaw calls it, as Lemkin disagrees with Shaw's concept of destruction as it pertains to genocide. In 1945, with the word genocide beginning to circulate, Lemkin wrote an article to explain the meaning of the genocide concept. He wrote, "The term does not necessarily signify mass killings although it may mean that. More often it refers to a coordinated plan aimed at destruction of the essential foundations of the life of national groups so that these groups wither and die like plants that have suffered a blight" (Frey 2009, 3). Obviously, the Palestinians certainly did not wither and die. In fact, it was the Jordanians and Egyptians, during their 19-year occupation of the disputed territories that caused a withering of the Palestinian society. It was only after the Israelis took control of that land that the Palestinians came out from under the thumb of Arab oppression and renewed their national ambitions.

Delving into the issue of population transfer – ethnic cleansing, claiming that the Zionists knew that this population transfer would likely require force, Shaw quickly labels it genocidal even though there is no proof of any desire to murder hundreds of thousands of Palestinians to achieve this movement. To state that such movement is "universally destructive," even if the means are not murderous on a large scale, seems to make no sense. How does such population movement "destroy everything?"

However, Shaw actually destroys his own argument with a story half way through his essay. He relays a story from Morris' *Revisiting the Palestinian Exodus of 1948,* about a discussion between the head of the international Zionist movement, Dr. Chaim Weizmann, and the Soviet Union's Ambassador to Great Britain as to "the prospects" of moving half a million of British Mandate Palestine's Arabs into neighboring Transjordan and its neighbor, Iraq (Shaw 2010, 13). There was, however, a caveat; the methods used by the Soviets to remove their own potential 5th column could not and would not (as the methods used were likely immoral) be used. While Shaw tries to backtrack, stating that the events of 1947-1949 might suggest that the Zionists disregarded Weizmann's caveats, the facts remain that the caveats held and that there is no valid comparison between the Soviet's genocidal exile of their Caucuses mountain tribes to Siberia, with the associated death of a quarter of the tribal population, and the Arab Diaspora during the Palestinian Civil War and subsequent Arab-Israeli war, wherein Israel and the Palestinians had an equivalent number of fatalities, approximately 6,000 people each.

Despite proof to the contrary, Shaw continues with his belief of an existing "genocidal mentality" within the Zionist leadership. He ridicules Pappé's use of the term "ethnic cleansing" by accusing him of using a Wikipedia definition and ignoring those who criticize the term (Strangely, here Shaw cites his own book, *What is Genocide*, published in 2007 while Pappé's tome was published in 2006). Additionally, Shaw's choice of words regarding Zionist rational decision making process regarding Arab violence, considering it "radicalizing," could hardly be more pejorative (Shaw 2010, 15).

Shaw's last attempt to conflate the ethnic cleansing of Bosnian Muslims with the Palestinian situation is untenable, just as Shaw admits that all comparison of the Palestinian Nakba to the Holocaust is untenable (Shaw 2010, 18). Shaw claims the death count in Bosnia, about 250,000, was not "legally" considered genocide because there was no proof that the intent was to murder all or even most Bosniaks. Indeed, most of the evidence points to the use of force solely for forced relocation purposes, not an effort to eradicate a people. However, Shaw contends that forced relocation is covered by Lemkin's definition of genocide as the intent was to destroy the community in the region. But that is not Lemkin's definition of Genocide. Indeed, the Bosnian community remains intact, just in another part of Bosnia.

William Schabas, one of the most prominent genocide scholars today, comments on this in a discussion about international law and genocide. In his paper concerning "A Legal Distinction between 'Genocide' 'War Crimes' and 'Crimes against Humanity,'" he questions the determination of genocide by any of the parties involved in the Bosnian conflict (Schabas 2006, 12). This action, in his opinion, was ethnic cleansing and rightfully charged as a crime against humanity. Apparently, the courts agreed with the defense attorneys, of those charged with genocide, over everything that occurred, other than in the case of the Srebrenica Massacre wherein about 8,000 prisoners were slaughtered over a three day period of time, being declared innocent of the charges. Again, in Schabas opinion, the massacre in Srebrenica should be classified as a micro- or mini-genocide (Schabas 2006, 12).

Finally, Shaw reveals his contempt for the term "ethnic cleansing." His first argument deals with the terminology used by the Croatian fascist party (Ustasha) leadership regarding the expulsion of the Serbs during WW II. Just as used by the Serbs to describe their expulsion of Bosniaks and Croats from Bosnia, Shaw finds fault in that it is the "perpetrator's term" and they should not have the right to label their crimes (Shaw 2007, 49). He claims that "expulsion" and "forced migration" are terms, already in use, that adequately describe what occurred. In this matter of semantics, he has a legitimate point. However, the Israeli government forcefully expelled the Jewish population of Gaza in 2005. Violence was used but no deaths were reported, at least none through government force. One could hardly say that Gaza was ethnically cleansed so it seems a legitimate term to use when a different ethnic group expels another, as so described by UN Special Rapporteur Tadeusz Mazowiecki (Shaw 2007, 50).

Several scholars also insist that ethnic cleansing, which might lead to genocide, is not genocide itself if there is no intention to wipe the group off the face of the Earth. Using this line of reasoning, the International Court of Justice denied Bosnia and Herzegovina's argument and despite the facts that the Serbs had deliberately cut off food supplies and had deliberately attempted to "eradicate all traces of the culture" of the Bosniaks, the mental element required to charge genocide was absent (Schabas 2009, 293).

Shaw's second argument takes into account the Zimbabwe attempt to cleanse the forest of the aftermath of death and destruction caused by the African Wars (Shaw 2007, 52-3). Here he makes a point, invalid though it may be, that cleansing should only be used to describe the act of removing dirt from an object, removing the results of evil from a landscape. However, that is hardly the meaning of the word "clean," and it is not for scholars to argue terminology which, if anything, will only confuse the average reader. Indeed, it is the classic Lewis Carroll's *Through the Looking Glass* argument that "when I use a word... it means just what I choose it to mean — neither more nor less" (Sabien 2015)

To cleanse is to remove a foreign object whether it be cars from a road, dogs from a park, or people from a region. There is nothing negative or positive about the word clean except within the context that it is being used.

### Palestine and Genocide: An International Historical Perspective
### Genocide Revisited

In 2013, after much critique and an exchange of emails between Shaw and Omer Bartov, a renowned Holocaust historian, along with an injudicious interjection by Israel Charney, Shaw revisited his 2010 paper. In this he revises, or updates, his theory to include the possibility that a combination of three elements, each enough to produce the genocidal affects in his earlier opinion, that formed the guiding force of the supposed genocide of the Arabs of British Mandate Palestine. These three elements; "settler colonialism," "Eastern European Nationalism," and "Decolonialism," all existed in the run up to Israeli independence. However, in almost the same breath, Shaw explains how each of these elements also limited the scope of the genocide.

Therefore, this seems to be a self-defeating strategy. The major episodes of war related genocides that are due to nationalistic zeal, notably the Holocaust and the Armenian Genocide, but also including the genocide of the Serbians by the Ustasha regime in the Nazi-sponsored state of Croatia, and the genocide of the Greeks and Assyrians during the Armenian Genocide, were conducted under the cover of a war that involved a large portion of the Earth, while the Palestinian wars were stand-alone regional conflicts that barely went beyond the borders of British Mandate Palestine.

Further, genocide could not possibly be a force derived from the settler colonialism of the Jews. First off, there was no colonization. Starting in the 1860s, Jews were not moving in, staking out land, and killing whoever stood in their way. They were buying land from the legal owners, often at a premium price. They were immigrating, sometimes illegally, into their own homeland, much the same as the return of the descendants of the 1840 Irish famine diaspora to the 1990 Ireland because of its amazing economic growth.

By the time of the UN partition vote, the Jews had bought 25% of the agrarian land. That the landless Arab tenant farmer feared being moved off the land was through the unfortunate natural consequence of not owning the land. That they chose to fight because they would lose control of what they never owned cannot be realistically blamed on the Jews. As for decolonization, the British, as the Mandate administrator, never truly controlled the Jewish society in British Mandate Palestine and the British certainly took the least amount of casualties possible prior to abandoning the fort. So in the case of Israel, settler-colonialism cannot be considered a genocidal force.

Shaw's final thrust in his essay actually centers on reasons why, in his opinion, Israel has not completed its genocidal designs, regardless of whether or not his theory is correct. It appears that Israel's supposed bloodthirstiness is only constrained by what is laughingly considered international good will that condones "its violence when it appears to have some connection with Israel's military security," knowing that support will vanish if it attempts to remove the rest of its 1.5 million Israeli Arab population (Shaw 2013, 7). So no matter what Israel does, it is a no win situation with Israel always characterized as desiring to commit genocide, restrained only by international opinion, which, if ever unvigilant, will unwittingly unleash Israel's genocidal might.

Indeed, with that caveat in his conclusion, Shaw again states that Israel will try to ethnically cleanse the rest of the Arabs out of Israel if the right conditions present itself. In his final paragraph, he writes:

"The only presently foreseeable circumstance in which genocide is likely to become, once again, a major theme in Israeli-Palestinian relations is if the Israeli campaign against Iran leads to war. Not only might an Israeli attack contain genocidal elements (for example, targeting groups of Iranian scientists along with nuclear facilities), but a serious Iranian counterattack on Israel could provide the cover the Israeli right needs to start implementing its wilder ideas of 'transfer'." (Shaw 2013, 7)

## Pappé Revisited

Aside from the ridiculous parenthesized statement that targeting Iranian scientists along with their nuclear facilities would constitute the crime of genocide, this unfortunate bit of logical fallacy was indulged in by Ilan Pappé during the build up to the second Gulf War. In a lecture presented by Pappé to the Right to Return Coalition – Al Awda UK, held at the School for Oriental and African Studies in London Monday 16th September 2002, he stated:

"We must all take the danger of a recurrence of the 1948 ethnic cleansing very seriously. This is not just paranoia when I directly – not indirectly – link the war against Iraq with the possibility of another Nakba.

Take it seriously, believe me. There is a serious Israeli conceptualization of the situation in which Israeli leaders say to themselves, 'we have a carte blanche from the Americans. The Americans will not only allow us to cleanse Palestine once and for all, they even will help create the window of opportunity for implementing our scheme. We will be condemned by the world, but this will be short-lived and eventually forgotten. This is a rare opportunity to 'solve' the problem.'" (M. Kramer 2002)

Of course, indulging in this type rhetoric is little more than pandering to an audience of "true believers" who would never think to question any prophecy that demonizes Israel. While there has never been a plan displayed that shows any kind of scenario wherein there is any mass expulsion of Arab-Israelis, which is hardly needed to convince an anti-Israel crowd. Both Shaw's and Pappé's concerns are not much more than the "wild anti-Israeli rhetoric" (Shaw 2013, 7) that they both ridicule and deride. When the prophecy failed to be fulfilled, the retort was, "perhaps because the consensus in the territories now is that Israel understands there's a limit to power" (M. Kramer 2002). This is just another nonsensical retort to a scenario that was invented out of whole cloth.

In this particular case, a rather scholarly attempt to reinvent genocide fails as easily as political attempts to do the same.

# Chapter Six

# New History and the New Catastrophe

In 2012, John Docker, the Honorary Professor in the School of Philosophical and Historical Inquiry at the University of Sydney, in the pages of the *Holy Land Journal*, claims that he follows Martin Shaw's determination, as in the 2010 article, that the Israeli's ethnic cleansing of the Palestinian Arabs in 1948 constituted an act of genocide, as discussed in the previous chapter. However, Docker does not actually follow Shaw, he precedes Shaw by 7 years.

In 2012, Docker merely reiterates his 2003 declaration; the removal of the majority of Arabs residing in the 78% of British Mandate Palestine that is now recognized as the state of Israel, by force and other means, was an act of genocide. Further, that the genocide committed against these Arabs, now commonly referred to as the Palestinians, continues unabated to this day. In his 2012 essay, as in 2003, Docker relies heavily on Ilan Pappé's material and his own interpretation of Raphael Lemkin's writings.

However, unlike Shaw's scholarly discourse, partially an academic exercise written to generate discussion as to the definition of genocide through exploring Lemkin's original works, in order to justify labeling Israel as genocidal, Docker desires to end any such discussion, as seen by his conclusions:

> Zionist Israel, from 1948 to the present, is guilty of geno-
> cidal acts as defined in Article II, in that it historically

> intended, and still intends, to destroy, in whole or in part, the Palestinians as a group… Furthermore, the worldwide Zionist organizations, along with the nations across the world, principally the United States, that support Zionist Israel in its genocidal acts, are guilty, in terms of Article III, of "complicity in genocide." (Docker 2012: 29)

With this conclusion, it becomes even clearer that Docker does not emulate Martin Shaw at all. After all, Shaw makes no judgment call regarding his findings, only that those findings should be further discussed. In this, while I believe him to be incorrect in his assessment, Shaw follows the educator's path of scholarly debate. Docker does not follow that path. Instead, it appears that Docker actually follows and emulates a controversial supporter of Palestinian supremacy, the international attorney and law professor, Francis A. Boyle, who seems to deal exclusively in rationalized political propaganda, rather than scholastic research, as previously shown in chapters four and five and will be shown in chapter ten.

In chapter two of this book, numerous academics; William Hewitt, Israel Charny, Leo Kuper, Helen Fein, and Barbara Harff among them; all acclaimed genocide scholars, provided their particular definitions of genocide and not one claims ethnic cleansing as genocidal on its own merits, as Docker so claims.

Again, as previously discussed, the term "genocide" is often misunderstood and thus misapplied. However, with Docker, it certainly seems to be a case of deliberate misapplication of the term, as has occurred with other controversial terms, such as "antisemitism." There are those whose efforts to distort the meaning of labels have been tried in the political attempt to lessen the charge of antisemitism. There are some, including a Nobel Laureate, who have inferred that Arabs cannot be antisemitic as they are a Semitic people (Tutu 2002; Zogby 2012; Walker 2013). Additionally, one well known and respected author has charged that the vast majority of Jews are not Semitic at all; rather they are descendants of the Khazars (Walker 2013). However, antisemitism, like genocide, is a coined word. The originator had a specific meaning in mind when coining the word. The word "antisemitism" was invented to differentiate the hatred of people practicing Judaism, Judeo-phobia, from the hatred of Jews as a distinct people. Therefore, it would not matter what any particular bigot believes concerning the ancestry of today's Jews, nor who is and is not a "Semite"; the bigots behavior remains antisemitic.

An example of Docker distorting the meaning of the word genocide in its legal context is illustrated in his opinion piece, co-authored with Ned Curthoys, in 2009 for Drum TV. Docker accuses Israel of committing genocide during the three week war with Gaza at the end of December 2008 (Docker and Curthoys 2009). However, Docker does not refer to the UN's definition that "Genocide is a denial of the right of existence of entire human groups, as homicide is the denial of the right to live of individual human beings" (UNGA 1946), which is the basis of the 1948 Genocide Convention. Instead, Docker states that he takes his meaning of genocide from Lemkin's 1944 book Axis Rule in Occupied Europe. How one decides to accuse someone of committing a crime by ignoring the definition of the crime in accordance with the law, in favor of a definition outside the legal field, is likely the same as charging someone with vehicular manslaughter who has merely jay-walked, purely on the basis of proximity to a car and a road.

But the UN is quite clear; genocide is to the group as murder is to the person. It is the murder of the group purely because of the identity of the group that "shocks the conscience of mankind" (UNGA 1946), not the collateral damage that occurs when attacking a group who deliberately place missile launching apparatus inside crowded residential areas.

One of Docker's stranger calls is for intellectual independence of the International Jewish community. However, in order to demonstrate such independency, the community must believe in what Docker believes. For example, this is Docker's demand of the Diaspora community in Australia regarding the Israeli-Palestinian conflict: "To attempt to regain honour and dignity, its autonomy, its self-respect, the Australian Diaspora has to recover intellectual independence. It has to say to Zionism and Israel: ..." (Docker 2003). In order to recover its intellectual independence, the Jewish community of Australia must state what Docker tells it to state?

On an interesting aside, Docker seems to know when not to bring up the notion that Israel committed genocide. Invited as a speaker at the Holocaust Museum in Washington, DC, Docker refrained from mentioning Israel during his lecture on *Raphael Lemkin's History of Genocide and Colonialism* in 2004, but he did manage to throw in Freud's belief that Judaism stems from Egyptian culture, that Yahweh was "originally a stranger to the Israelites, an Arab Midianite god" (Docker 2004).

## Nakba Memoricide: Genocide Studies and the Zionist/Israeli Genocide of Palestine

In 2014, Docker revisited his genocidal claims with the assistance of Haifa Rashed and Dr. Damian Short, both associated with the University of London's Human Rights Consortium. Docker begins by issuing the usual baseless caveat, blaming the lack of academic discussion over the founding of Israel through an act of genocide being due to a fear of "becoming another victim of Zionist intimidation and retaliatory attacks" (Rashed, Short and Docker 2014, 2). However, as shown by the conversation between Martin Shaw and Omar Bartov over Shaw's paper concerning the possibility of expanding the definition of genocide to cover ethnic cleansing wherein Israel Charny made such an inappropriate attack, Charny's chastisement by the head of the International Association of Genocide Scholars, as well as the lack of support for Charny's accusations against Shaw, should have laid that canard to rest (Beckerman 2011). Additionally, the fact that no other genocide scholar has taken Shaw to task regarding an academic notice of antisemitic remarks easily dismisses Docker's concerns. Regardless, Docker continues in that vein (Rashed, Short and Docker 2014, 13).

Docker presents a two page case study (Rashed, Short and Docker 2014, 5-6) wherein he discusses the numerous papers and books by prominent genocide scholars who for some strange reason find no need to include the plight of the Palestinians in any of their works. Amazingly, Docker comes up with a term to describe that massive collective effort, surely obvious (conspiracy?), to not mention the Nakba. This is clearly, according to Docker, "memoricide;" the deliberate effort to remove an event from history, or better known in Palestinian propaganda circles as "Nakba Denial."

Docker stresses Lemkin's intellectual dissection of genocide wherein it is considered accomplished when the "destruction of the national pattern of the oppressed group;" is followed by "the imposition of the national pattern of the oppressor." However, Docker does not explain how this type of activity has any relevance to Israel nor why this type of activity could possibly be labeled "the crime of crimes" or be seen in the same light as the murder of about 8,000 Bosniak prisoners in three days in Srebrenica, the murder of 450,000 Hungarian Jews in Auschwitz in three weeks, or the slaughter of 800,000 Tutsis in 100 days in Rwanda.

To make matters more confusing, Docker also decided to rework Lemkin's definition of *genos* so rather than the term referring to a distinct people, for Docker it refers to practitioners of a distinct culture. Of course, Lemkin did include a cultural aspect to groups of people that would fall under the category of victims, but he did not define what made one culture different than another. For example, the Arabs of Ramallah had different customs than the Arabs of Bethlehem, but they were of the same cultural background. However, additional misuse of such definitions could have someone seeing genocide occurring in most any area of cultural change, such as when a large influx of immigrants from one culture settles in another area. One could say the change in the culture initiated by the influx of Somali refugees into a small town in Minnesota is an imposition and forced change from that of the now put upon inhabitants, some whose families have lived there for over 200 years. An even greater change was the Arabizing of the Palestinian region from 700 CE onward. Is this forced change a form of genocide? Far from it. Further, consider the fictitious "right of return" demanded by the Palestinians. Would this not be an imposition of a Palestinian or an Arab "culture" on what would soon become the minority Jewish population? It is fairly obvious that Lemkin had conflicting ideas on the exact definition of genocide but it is likely this was not one of those ideas.

Another issue regarding Docker's changing definitions deals with his insistence that the study of such requires the shift of genocide from a legal term to a discursive one. Docker believes "we should not base the historical study of genocide on a legal definition alone; indeed, we should not base the historical study of any phenomena on a legal definition alone" (Docker 2010). But this is as illogical as conducting a study of the history of murder without utilizing its legal definition, thus inferring that anytime one person kills another through any means, including the most benign of negligence, it is murder.

Docker brings Pappé's Ethnic Cleansing of Palestine back into the picture with a discussion of Mark Levene's review of the book. Docker stresses Levene's statement regarding the importance of Pappé's book for scholars researching genocide and its suboptimal variants. However, Docker misinterprets the importance Levene assigns to genocide scholars, for Pappé's analysis is not a study of genocide but of ethnic cleansing, an action regarding the removal of a people that does not rise to the level of genocide. In other words, the actions committed by Israel during the Palestinian Civil War and subsequent Arab-Israeli war, is a clear example of the difference between genocide and ethnic cleansing. Indeed, there may be no record anywhere of so many people taken out of their homes and lands with so little loss of life. This is Levene's cue to genocide scholars doing comparative studies.

Levene stresses that the relevance with this episode of ethnic cleansing's similarity with genocide solely rest with the notion of a directing central planning authority (Levene 2007, 677). Docker's objection is that Levene refutes Pappé's allegation that this cleansing was always in play as a viable plan since the advent of political Zionism in 1897. Indeed, the Jews persuaded the "Druze, Caucasians, and Bedouins to "act against their own supposed "national" interest (Levene 2007, 680). Were these also not the indigenous to be removed to make Israel supposedly "demographically viable?"

While there was always discussion on how the existing Arab population would react to the increasing Jewish population, the Arab riots during the 1936-39 time frame ended the discussion. After those years, there was no question as to what the general Arab reaction would be when the Jews eventually took control of a portion of British Mandate Palestine. But Docker ignores those conclusions. Docker, like Pappé, fails to mention that over 1200 Jews had been murdered by Arabs between the UNGA partition vote and Israel's declaration of independence (Frantzman 2008).

Docker ends his discussion of Levene's review with Levene's remark that "The injustice of the Nakba, all these years on, is of ongoing relevance – just as much as the Armenian genocide..." (Docker 2013 7). As this was part of a block quote, it is worth examining why Docker did not enclose the quote in its entirety. That examination reveals that the total sentence actually negates Docker's point in the discussion. Levene actually states, "The injustice of the Nakba, all these years on, is of ongoing relevance – just as much as the Armenian genocide, or any other event which, however hidden or dissembled about, is founded on mass violence" (Levene 2007 680). Docker hopes to relay that the "Nakba" should be studied as a genocide, but Levene states that it should be studied as an event in which violence changed the course of international relations and as Turkey, trying to enter the European Union, will always be beset about its denial of the Armenian Genocide and its failure to attempt any kind of reconciliation. Likewise, Israel must come clean about the ethnic cleansing of British Mandate Palestine, along with a meaningful reconciliation process, to be accepted in the region. However, there is nothing noted that indicates that there is anything Israel can do, short of disappearing, that will result in Israel being accepted in the region. Just as it is likely nothing Turkey can do, other than stop being Turkey, which will convince the European states to accept Turkey into the European Union, the Armenian Genocide issue is just a convenient stumbling block.

As in Docker's previous papers, it appears his ultimate goal is to find an academic path toward proving Israel committed genocide in 1948 and continues to commit genocide through today. And as in his previous papers, that determination requires going back to interpreting Lemkin's

1944 definition of genocide rather than the UN's definition in 1946 and the various types as defined in the 1948 Genocide Convention.

Revisiting his conclusion, Docker blames his "fellow scholars'" cowardice on their fear of being called names through "Zionist intimidation and ad hominem attacks" (Docker 2013, 13). Of course, being called names doesn't scare Docker. In fact, it does not seem to scare anyone at all. It appears to be just another canard in the antisemite and/or anti-Zionist's arsenal.

Consider the late Edward W. Said, a noted professor of English at Columbia University and the author of *Orientalism*, of whom no one is ever likely to say was a friend to Israel or that he was concerned about what anyone called him. In his afterword in Ragan and Shlaim's *The War for Palestine*, he describes himself of having been spared the horror of being forced out of the Palestinian territories by leaving in December of 1947, as many other elites did, and returning to their family home in Cairo. At no time does Said refer to the Palestinian exile as a holocaust, nor as being genocidal. In fact, Said provides an answer to those who now claim so; "Over time it is the distortions that are increased, not the reality of the language" (Said 2001, 214).

Another example of a writer with no fear of attack is Rashid Khalidi, a New Yorker of Palestinian-Lebanese descent who is also the Edward W. Said Professor of Modern Arab Studies at Columbia University and author of *The Iron Cage*. Again, no one can claim him as a friend to Israel, yet there is nothing in his most famous history of the Palestinians referring to a genocide of the Palestinians (R. Khalidi 2006, 267-281).

In fact, the list of those authors who apparently could not care less about being called an antisemite, yet do not identify the events of 1948 as being a genocide, is quite notable. That list includes the aforementioned Said and Khalidi as well as; Avi Shlaim, Phylis Bennis, Christopher Hitchens, Barbara Coloroso, Robert Fisk, Nicholas Guyattand Sami Hadawi, among many, many others.

It is ironic that Docker accuses genocide scholars who do not agree with him as not doing so purely for political reasons: "Genocide Studies is now on the edge of an ethical precipice, a crisis of intellectual bad faith, claiming to be making scholarly choices only, when those choices are subtended by political considerations (Rashed, Short and Docker 2014, 13). However, it appears that it is political concern alone that drives Docker to accuse Israel of genocide.

# Chapter Seven

# Slouching Toward a Palestinian Holocaust?

Richard Falk, American Professor Emeritus of international law at Princeton University and former special rapporteur on Palestinian human rights for the United Nations Human Rights Council, has a sordid history regarding his relationship with Israel. Not one for diplomatic language, Falk has, on numerous occasions, wildly charged Israel with planning and committing genocide.

In 2007, Falk wrote an essay implying that Israel's treatment of the Palestinian people can be justifiable compared to the Nazi Holocaust. While this comparison on face value alone seems absurd, Falk opens with a description of the Nazi atrocity as being "as close to unconditional evil as has been revealed throughout the entire bloody history of the human species. Its massiveness, unconcealed genocidal intent, and reliance on the mentality and instruments of modernity give its enactment in the death camps of Europe a special status in our moral imagination" (Falk 2007).

Falk ponders on whether or not it is irresponsible to label Israel's activities as having reached that standard of evil, but he then decides it is quite appropriate when his imagining of the Israeli mindset is taken into consideration. As part of Falk's justification, he believes that Israel is deliberately subjecting the entirety of Gaza's population to "life-endangering conditions of utmost cruelty" (Falk 2007)

This particular essay has been cited in the condemnations associated with Falk's appointment to a position wherein objective judgment must be used to determine if Israel is acting legally, regarding the safeguarding of the human rights of Palestinians in the Israeli militarily-controlled Palestinian territories. The Israeli ambassador stated:

> It was impossible to believe that out of a list of 184 potential candidates, the eminently wise members of the Consultative Group honestly had made the best possible choice for this post. In a recent article, the proposed candidate (Falk) stated that he did not think it was "an irresponsible overstatement to associate the treatment of Palestinians with the criminalized Nazi record of collective atrocity". Someone who had publicly and repeatedly stated such views could not possibly be considered independent, impartial or objective, as was explicitly required in the institution building text. The Human Rights Council was rapidly moving away from its *raison d'être*. The members of the Council were missing an opportunity to show the world that this Human Rights Council genuinely sought improvement, the chance to make a difference, and the prospect of laying the groundwork for better cooperation with Israel. (UN 2008)

Another ambassador, Marius Grinius of Canada, stated "Based on the writings of one of the candidates (Falk)... Canada expressed serious concern about whether the high standards established by the council would be met by this individual. Therefore, Canada dissociated itself from any council decision to approve the full slate" (Lungen, 2008).

Throughout Falk's tenure with the UNHRC, he has been castigated by representatives of liberal democracies. In 2013, the US representative, Ambassador Eileen Chamberlain Donahoe, sent this missive:

> The United States completely rejects the provocative and offensive commentary by Mr. Richard Falk, UN Special Rapporteur for the Palestinian Territories, regarding the recent terrorist attack in Boston, Massachusetts.

We have repeatedly called for Mr. Falk's resignation and expressed our grave concern in a letter to the UN High Commissioner for Human Rights (Excerpt: "Special Rapporteurs are supposed to be impartial, objective, and demonstrate personal integrity. Mr. Falk's behavior is not consistent with these qualities, and his lack of judgment… is stunning.") Mr. Falk's continued offensive communications do nothing to advance peace in the Middle East or to further the protection and promotion of human rights. Mr. Falk's latest comments demonstrate once again that he is unfit to serve in his role as a UN special rapporteur. (UN Watch 2013)

In 2014, Falk unknowingly admitted to his complete bias regarding the Arab-Israeli conflict in an interview he gave on Democracy Now – "But as I've said all along, you only have to be 10 percent objective to come to the same critical conclusions that I came to in relation to Israel's violation of fundamental human rights in the West Bank, East Jerusalem and Gaza…" (Falk 2014b).

Falk describes horrific conditions that do not seem to exist in Gaza except in his viewpoint. How are the living conditions in Gaza life endangering? The population of Gaza increased from 350,000 in 1970 (McCarthy 2001) to 1.85 million in 2015 (CIA 2016). Where in Nazi -occupied Europe did any Jewish population anywhere grow by any means other than by Nazi directed population movements with the intention of keeping greater numbers of Jews penned up prior to slaughter? In Gaza, life expectancy went from 44 in 1970 to 74 in 2015 (CIA 2016). Where in Nazi-occupied Europe did the life expectancy of Jews increase?

As an indication of Falk's lack of good intention in this matter, he seriously forwarded Hamas offer to consider accepting Israel's existence if Israel agreed to return to the pre-Six-Day War borders, which is, for the Israeli government, a ludicrous position and not one legally required by any international organization (Falk 2016). Further proof of Falk's inability to view any aspect of the Israeli-Palestinian conflict objectively are the several condemnations, including calls for his resignation or dismissal, he has garnered from the UN Secretary General, several UN Ambassadors from Canada and the United States, as well as Israel, for his inflammatory antisemitic, and conspiracy-related remarks.

### We Called it Genocide in Guatemala. Why Not in Gaza Too?

Another who has conflated the third Gaza War with genocide is Patricia Davis, writing in *Foreign Policy in Focus*, supporting Palestinian President Abbas' accusation of such (Davis 2014). Davis claims that rather than compare the situation in Gaza with the Holocaust, Rwanda, or Bosnia, it is proper to compare it to the genocide in Guatemala wherein the military murdered 5.5% of the indigenous Ixil Maya population in the 1980s (Davis 2014, 2). Of course, a casualty rate that high in Gaza would have meant about 100,000 dead but that is not the point. As always, the point is political.

The relationship between the two events comes to population control as Davis refers to a quote from Jane Hunter intimating that the Palestinian population is not allowed to exceed the Jewish population, and that this is official Israeli policy justifying genocide. On the Guatemalan side, she states that the military wanted to reduce the Mayans to a minority (Hunter 1987).

Davis also charges Israeli politicians for inciting genocide, which is actually a crime. Strangely and hypocritically, Davis makes these accusations against Israeli officials for identifying Palestinian leaders who incite genocide in their Mosques and schools. Of course, Davis conveniently forgets Julius Streicher, the chief propagandist for Nazi Germany, who was executed for the same type of incitement broadcasted by these Palestinian leaders (Holocaust Encyclopedia 2015).

Finally, Davis equates Israel's action in Gaza to the Guatemalan military's practice of herding the Mayans into churches and schools, locking the doors, and setting the buildings on fire (Davis 2014, 4). The absolute ridiculousness of such a comparison is astounding and requires anyone believing such a notion to have suspended their sense of disbelief.

### Never again! European collusion in Israel's slow genocide

Omar Barghouti, founder of the controversially antisemitic BDS move-ment, rides the Falk genocide-accusation bandwagon with his editorial in Electronic Intifada, not only accusing Israel of committing genocide in Gaza, but also accusing the European Union, and the United States, of being complacent and uncaring about it, if not actually and actively encouraging Israel's genocidal behavior. Like Falk, Barghouti accuses Israel of committing a slow genocide through depriving Gazans of clean water, sewage treatment, and electrical power. Barghouti claims that this is Israel's deliberate plan "to kill, cause serious bodily and mental harm, and deliberately inflict conditions of life calculated to bring about partial and gradual physical destruction [which] qualifies as an act of genocide, if not all-out genocide yet" (Barghouti 2008).

Additionally, like Falk, Barghouti does not provide any proof or num-bers demonstrating any objective international institutional body to have any reason to believe anything remotely close to genocide has ever oc-curred in the Palestinian territories, let alone in Gaza itself.

# Chapter Eight

# As if Americans did not know

Alison Weir (not the British author of historical fiction with the same name), one of the shallowest and most adamant anti-Israel speakers and writers around, is the founder of an anti-Israel organization pejoratively called "If Americans Knew." Weir's premise is that most Americans are ignorant about the Arab-Israeli conflict and that she is dedicated to educating these supposedly ignorant Americans as to Israel's conduct in the Middle East through posting and promoting what has been characterized as "outrageous accusations with absolute conviction" (Stand4facts 2005) and exposing the support given by the US government that is, in her opinion, against American national interest. Of course Weir's basic failure is the inability to recognize that America's greatness is reflected in its national values, such as the unwavering commitment to supporting liberal democracies, and not just its national interest which is usually confined to security and economics.

In Weir's latest campaign, promoted in 2015, she complains about being accused of anti-semitism, which is not an unreasonable accusation concerning her many pejorative statements and accusations (Weir 2015a; 2015b). Both Jewish Voices for Peace (JVP 2015) and the American Palestinian solidarity umbrella organization, US Campaign to End the Israeli Occupation (End The Occupation 2015), have ended their relationship with Weir over her blatant antisemitism and her pandering to white supremacist organizations and individuals.

When queried as to being pro-Israel or pro-Palestinian, Weir claims that:

> (she) found that question off-putting because it's not a football game and it's not a matter of being on one side or the other but of being true to the facts and sensitive to injustice in whatever form. That said, it didn't take someone trained in linguistics to figure out which side she was on. (Applebome 2008)

As with much of her writing, she usually relies on rumor, innuendo, and half-truth to make her points. Here is one such example: Weir wrote a book about the involvement of the US in the re-creation of Israel. On the cover, Weir uses what she claims to be a 1947 quote from Dean Acheson, a very influential statesmen in both the Roosevelt and Truman administrations, concerning the creation of Israel (Weir 2014, cover). However, not only was the quoted portion stated in 1945 and not in 1947, the actual quote had little to do with the creation of Israel, a name not in use until 1948. For the most part, it dealt with the Jewish refugee issue and settlement in British Mandate Palestine (Acheson 1969, 169). A second example: Weir claims that she has proof that Israelis know that calling someone an antisemite is a trick (Weir 2013), however, her sole source references a 2002 interview with an elderly, retired, and very liberal former member of the Israeli government (Weir 2013). The interview was conducted by an ultra-leftwing organization (Democracy Now) and broadcast on fringe TV and radio stations, and the former MK was giving her unqualified opinion, as she provided no proof. A third example: Weir constantly harps on being the subject of death threats (Weir 2015a). Again, her sole source is a list of one item, the only known threat from 13 years ago (Weir 2003). How that single episode morphed into multiple threats is anyone's guess. While Weir claims that her critics are "misrepresenting the facts using filtered, misleading statements, spin, negative innuendo, and outright falsehoods" (Weir 2015c), it is easily proven that she is quite adept at doing exactly what she describes her critics are doing and that her opponents are not misrepresenting her opinions at all.

Finally, when taking the American Historical Association (AHA) to task over their refusal to accept advertising for her aforementioned somewhat fictional history book about America's role in the creation of Israel, she referenced in her defense, which is no longer on her website but still (as of this writing) on her "Facebook" page (Knew 2015), an article from the self-described "investigative historian," Eric Zuesse. Weir calls him as a "real" historian. I assume this is merely returning the compliment as Zuesse states, in showing his contempt for the AHA, "I happen not to be a member of that association; but, if I were, I would quit in disgust. She is a historian; they are not" (Zuesse 2015). An internet search showed no relevant background for Zuesse, no source of training and no recorded education. However, there are some unusual books (self-published?) to Zuesse's credit including one with a unique theory as to why Hitler wanted the Holocaust to occur (Zuesse 2000). Additionally, he has made numerous contributions to a variety of online magazines; some reputable, some not.

*But this is not an expose of* Alison Weir and her particular brand of "journalism", this chapter deals with Weir's accusation that Israel is committing genocide, both in her writing and in what she posts on her web site. In 2004, Weir wrote, regarding interviews she conducted in the Palestinian territories, "I listened to old people who described the start of this holocaust..." and "They described what it was like when three-quarters (75%) of your entire population is ethnically cleansed (*in actuality, only 60% of those originally qualified to be called "refugees" left and of those, half that figure moved to other portions of the Palestinian region – author's note* )," and finally, "... one of the most massive and brutal displacements of a people in modern times..." (Weir 2004). When questioned about her supposed fanaticism, she retorts, "It is hard not to sound fanatic, overwrought, biased. The lie is too big, the repression too complete... to write about reasonably" (Stand4facts.org 2005).

Weir's terminology is certainly pejorative, but that is expected in what can only be described as propaganda. It is routine in fanatic anti-Israel

literature to ascribe Nazi imagery to the acts committed by Jews during the Palestinian Civil War, which was started by the Palestinian Arabs,
not the Palestinian Jews, and the acts committed by the nascent Israeli
Defense Force during the subsequent Arab-Israeli War started by the five
Arab Armies that invaded the Palestinian region.

However, declaring that the losing side of that particular civil war underwent a holocaust, is rather far reaching. Equally far reaching is the
declaration that this action was one of the most massive and brutal displacements of a people in modern times. Of course, we have no idea
what Alison Weir means when she says "modern times." For argument's
sake, let us consider the modern time starts with the year 1900.

From 1904 through 1907, the Germans colonizing Southwest Africa
(Namibia) murdered upwards of 60,000 Herero and 10,000 Nama as
they drove out a combined 100,000 indigenous tribesmen from the land.
From 1915 through 1923, the Ottoman Turks murdered upwards of 1.5
million Armenians while driving out approximately 3 million Armenians.
Upwards of a million Greeks and Assyrians were also dealt death as they
were driven from the homes they inhabited for centuries in Turkey. During
"The Holocaust," Germans and their allies murdered upwards of 6 million
Jews, at least an additional 5 million non-Jews, and displaced millions
of people from 1933 through 1945. From 1945, the ethnic cleansing of
about 12 million ethnic Germans from Poland and Czechoslovakia left
upwards of 2 million dead. The ethnic cleansing that accompanied the
partition of India into Hindu and Muslim (Pakistan) states left millions
dead. The 1972 genocide in Bangladesh consumed upwards of 3 million
Bangladeshi. Approximately 200,000 men, women, and children died in
the East Timor genocide which started in 1975. Upwards of two million
died in the Cambodian genocide starting in 1975. The 1982 genocide
of the Guatemalans saw upwards of 150,000 dead and one million displaced. The 1988 genocide of the Kurds by Iraq saw upwards of 200,000
deaths. The ethnic cleansing of Bosniaks in 1993-95 saw upwards of
250,000 killed and 2 million displaced. The 1994 Rwandan genocide saw
800,000 Tutsis murdered. While the list is far from complete, I will end it

with the 2003 genocide of Black African Darfur with up to 400,000 dead and millions driven off their land (Totten 2013).

Twelve episodes of major genocides and ethnic cleansing, not to mention the significant episodes of massacres such in Sri Lanka (Tamils), Central African Republic, Nigeria/Biafra (Ibos), Chechnya, and at least a dozen other locales that, comparatively, make the Palestinian episode appear to be little but a blip. As Martin Shaw earlier assured us, about 5,000 (combatant and non-combatant) Palestinian Arabs died during the Palestinian Civil War and subsequent First Arab-Israeli War. This is not to say that every innocent death is not a tragedy, but when someone claims that the Nakba was "one of the most massive and brutal displacements of a people in modern times," there must be some context in which to make the comparison. Obviously, Alison Weir is grossly exaggerating. But then, later on, Weir writes about the aftermath of a suicide bombing, reporting that the New York Times story covering the event wrote "a few paragraphs about Israeli crowds beating random Palestinian Israelis to a pulp – one was almost killed – and chanting 'Kill Arabs'" (Weir 2004). However, there was nothing in the story about anyone chanting, "Kill Arabs" nor anything about "beating random Palestinian-Israelis to a pulp" (Sontag 2001). So is Weir exaggerating or just lying? Perhaps Weir is merely "misrepresenting the facts using filtered, misleading statements, spin, negative innuendo, and outright falsehoods" (Weir 2015c).

It would seem that the investigative reporters at discoverthenetworks. org are correct when they state, "Weir's inflammatory assertions and distortions are matched only by her lack of information about the history of Israel and of the conflict" (Stand4facts.org 2005).

Of note is the recent upheaval within the American Palestinian solidarity movement wherein organizations and coalitions are removing Weir and her organization from their membership rolls (Horowitz 2015). It appears that Weir has been associating with antisemitic and white supremacist groups and individuals, which in turn alters the perception of the Palestinian Solidarity Movement away from mere independence and into racist politics. One of Weir's major defender, the noted antisemite Gilad Atzmon, does Weir no favor with his zealous defense (Atzmon 2015).

### Does it really Matter what you call it?

Alison Weir not only posts her own work on her site, she also posts anti-Israel essays from other authors. On the genocide accusation front, Weir posted an article by Kathleen and Bill Christison, who are both former CIA employees (Christison 2006). In an aside, Weir specifically states that Kathleen Christison is a "top author" concerning Israel's foundation (Weir, Against Our Better Judgment. 2014, i-ii) Their opening remarks deal with the same odious comparison of German Nazis to Israelis that Weir believes to be appropriate to use in her own writing. Further on, the Christisons discuss an attack on a member of the International Solidarity Movement (ISM), which is an extremist Palestinian support movement. They complain that no news organization reported the incident. It appears that the "victim" actually instigated the incident, so that it was truly not newsworthy. Indeed, a letter sent to the Swedish Ambassador seems to indicate that what the Christisons' reported was hardly accurate (Wilder 2006).

The Christisons' definition of what constitutes genocide is equally inaccurate. They offer William Cook's (a professor of English, hardly a qualification of note for an expert on genocide) article, the *Rape of Palestine,* as their guideline as to what constitutes genocide. Incredibly, Cook convolutedly waters down the definition of genocide to any "non-lethal act(s) that undermine[d] the liberty, dignity, and personal security of members of a group... if they contributed to weakening the viability of the group" (Cook 2006). Essentially, by Cook's definition, any action taken against any individual Palestinian, by the Israelis, is an act of genocide.

Cook's lack of veracity is demonstrated in one short part of the same story wherein he accuses Ariel Sharon of a "blatant desecration of the Al Aqsa Mosque with his entourage of 1000 IDF soldiers..." (Cook 2006), which is nonsensical as Sharon never entered, nor intended to enter, the mosque, he simply strode the grounds of the Temple Mount, an area sacred to Jews and, regardless of whether or not it was provocative, it was well within his right as an Israeli citizen to walk those grounds.

Actually, none of the Christisons' claims regarding Israel committing genocide can be considered factual. And it is no wonder that their charges, like William Cook's, are posted in places such as CounterPunch, a webzine noted for its antisemitic content (Livik 2012), and Weir's collection of outlandish anti-Israel material; They are not fit for mainstream media.

Another genocide accusation published on Weir's site is written by Sam Bahour and Michael Dahan. That article states that Israel is committing "symbolic genocide." While Bahour and Dahan take their definition of genocide from a dictionary, they refer to Professor Grinberg's, of Ben Gurion University, definition of symbolic genocide;

> Every people has its symbols, national leaders and political institutions, a home land, past and future generations, and hopes. All these symbolically represent a people. Israel is systematically damaging, destroying and eradicating all of these, with unbelievable bureaucratic jargon." (Bahour 2004)

What is more, Bahour and Dahan are not satisfied with the charge of genocide as the ultimate accusation. They end their article with their stance that even the accusation of genocide "seems too accommodating for such arrogance of power" (Bahour 2004). Amazing! The accusation that Israel committed genocide, the crime of crimes, is too mild. Perhaps Bahour and Dahan already realized that repeated inappropriate use of the term genocide weakens it tremendously and it can no longer reflect the true heinousness of Israel's crimes.

From all of this, it is rather obvious that Weir's accusations, and those of whom she promotes, are the least scholarly and the most propagandist of the lot.

# Chapter Nine

# The Electronic Intifada

Like the founder and editor of "If Americans Knew," the *Electronic Intifada* (*EI*), and its co-founder and editor, Ali Abunimah, specializes in providing material for the Palestinian solidarity movement's propaganda war against Israel (Bigman 2014b). Abunimah subscribes to an "Orwellian definition" of antisemitism to aid him in describing himself as opposing antisemitism while still espousing a rabid form of Jew-hatred (Bigman 2014a). The publication has been described as "cyberpropaganda," designed to show the Palestinian side of the story but in a manner so prejudicial as to be of little mainstream use (Sedan 2001).

Therefore, it is of no surprise that *EI* published Marwan Hassib Barghouti's 2002 54-count indictment of Israel, even while he was undergoing trial in Israeli courts for the crime of murder. Barghouti, as his own legal authority, indicted Israel for the crime of genocide, among other war crimes, and crimes against humanity (M. H. Barghouti 2002). Of course, no court accepted the charges, but that is not what propaganda is about.

In 2004, Nigel Perry, a co-founder of *EI*, wrote an article accusing US politicians, Israeli officials, comedian Jackie Mason, US charitable institutions, and CNN for either calling for genocide of the Palestinian people or failing to report genocide against the Palestinian people (Perry 2004). The time period covered by the accusation was for the time covering the second intifada, when 950 Israelis were murdered by Palestinians, many via Palestinian human bombs. That was not noted in the article. It is interesting to note that during the same time, 101 Palestinians were murdered by Palestinians due to suspicion of collaborating with Israel (BBC 2005). Again, that was also missing from Perry's article.

In 2006 and 2007, *EI* published Ilan Pappé's declarations that Israel is committing genocide in Gaza. Pappé's 2006 prediction that about 2600 Arabs would be killed by Israeli action in Gaza failed to pan out. As indicated by B'Tselem's (a pro-Palestinian NGO) pronouncement of the total number of Palestinians killed being 606 (Pappé 2007), presumably by the Israeli Government, in the entirety of the Israeli controlled territories. This did not appear to affect Pappé's faith in his obviously non-existent clairvoyant powers. Instead, he goes from "hesitat(ing) a lot before using this very charged term (genocide)," to "(I) came back to employing it today with even stronger conviction" (Pappé 2007). Rather than apologizing for his earlier incorrect assessment of the situation in Gaza, he doubled down.

In an interesting aside, it appears that Pappé recanted his accusation, for a short period of time, when he joined in on a letter addressed to the "international community" to make certain demands of Israel. This letter, written by a group of genocide scholars belonging to either of the international genocide scholars' organizations, the International Association of Genocide Scholars (IAGS) and the International Network of Genocide Scholars (INoGS), accused Israel of behavior that is "alarmingly close" to genocide (Brown 2009). "Alarmingly close" is not an accusation of having committed genocide. That Pappé signed this letter indicates one of two reasons; 1. Pappé realizes that Israel has never actually committed genocide or, 2. Pappé wanted to add his name to an actual group of noted scholars as his reputation is not that of such.

Regardless of motivation, it certainly does appear that Pappé deserves his reputation as a scholar that puts his political agenda before his commitment to scholarship.

In 2008, *EI* published Omar Barghouti's (a relative of the aforementioned Marwan Barghouti and a major player in the game of BDS) accusation that Europe is colluding with Israel's "slow genocide" of the Palestinians (Barghouti 2008). In this instance, Barghouti is seemingly upset that the international community is not even bothering to "lift a finger" and that the UN is merely paying "lip service," all the while Israel's "hermetic siege of

Gaza, designed to kill, cause serious bodily and mental harm, and deliber-ately inflict conditions of life calculated to bring about partial and gradual physical destruction" continues unabated (Barghouti 2008).

As with Pappé's charges, truth has been sacrificed for the sake of form. Additionally, it should be noted that Barghouti also charges the US, the Palestinian Authority, and the Arab League as accessories to the crime of genocide. However, he holds his greatest contempt for Europe, charging the continental power with attempting to reap redemption for the Holocaust by allowing the harvest of Palestinians. To further his argument, Barghouti also claims that Europe allows this harvest because it harbors a white racist ideology, that "Palestinians… do not count for much, as we are viewed…as lesser, or relative, humans" (O. Barghouti 2008).

Also in 2008, Ali Abunimah derided Israeli Deputy Defense Minister Vilnai statement, "the more Qassam [rocket] fire intensifies and the rock-ets reach a longer range, [the Palestinians] will bring upon themselves a bigger *shoah* because we will use all our might to defend ourselves" (Abunimah 2008). Of course, it appears that most parties missed the part where Vilnai mentioned a "bigger" event, indicating that the Palestinians were attempting to bring upon the Israelis a *shoah*. Additionally, as men-tioned in Chapter Four, *Shoah* (capitalized) is the Hebrew word used in lieu of the word Holocaust, specifically identifying the genocide of the Jewish people by Nazi Germany and many of their allies from 1933 to 1945. The word *shoah* (un-capitalized) is just a common word for disaster, just as *nakba* is a common Arabic word for catastrophe.

Ilan Pappé makes his genocidal accusation again in 2013 but it is even more incredulous than his accusations made in 2006 and 2007. This time he defames the former prime minister and former president of Israel, the Nobel Peace Laureate Shimon Peres. This accusation is based on what Pappé calls the "criminality of Peres' narrative which is as horrific as the occupation — and potentially far worse" (Pappé 2013) which happens to be that Peres gave a speech wherein he praised Israel's successes, returning to the land after a 1000+ year diaspora, but did not mention that there happened to be Arabs living on the land.

Again, Pappé makes all of the classic mistakes of a poor historian for which he holds a well-deserved reputation. Pappé faults Peres for perpetuating the "land without people" myth when the actual well-known phrase is "a land without a people." Not just people but a viable national group. As part of Ottoman Syria for 400 years, the Arabs residing there considered themselves to be Syrians, not Palestinians. Further, there was little thought or organization of an Arab Palestinian nationalistic movement until the advent of political Zionism.

For this "sin", Pappé considers Peres to have "already eliminated most of the Palestinians. If you did not exist when Peres came to Palestine, you definitely do not exist when he is the president in 2013. This elimination is the point where ethnic cleansing becomes genocidal" (Pappé 2013).

2013 through 2015 provides a litany of pieces published by *EI*; Contraception provided to Ethiopian Jews was genocidal in nature, Moshe Feiglan's genocidal plan for Gaza, the accusation about Hamas and child sacrifice encourages genocide, a 2014 Pappé piece once again accusing Israel of incremental genocide, so on and so forth (Electronic Intifada 2015).

What is important to remember is that *EI* produces propaganda designed to feed the choir that has a hatred for all things associated with Israel. The material, rarely accurate, does not have to be accurate. A case in point is illustrated by the international human rights attorney Michael Ratner (also described as President Emeritus of the Center for Constitutional Rights in New York and Chair of the European Center for Constitutional and Human Rights in Berlin) quoted on July 27, 2014 stating: "There's no doubt again here this is 'incremental genocide', as Ilan Pappé says. It's been going on for a long time, the killings, the incredibly awful conditions of life, the expulsions that have gone on for from (sic) Lydda in 1947 and '48, when 700 or more villages in Palestine were destroyed..." (Ratner 2014). Here is the same information from the same Michael Ratner, one month later stating: "But you can't look at this as an isolated attack on Gaza because there's a history going back to Zionists charting out and destroying five hundred plus villages in 1947-48..."

(Khalek 2014). So what is the number of villages allegedly destroyed? 500 plus? 700 plus?

In actuality, the consensus number agreed upon by most historians is number less than 500. In 2002, Palestinian-American artist Emily Jacir designed the *Memorial to 418 Palestinian Villages which were Destroyed, Depopulated and Occupied by Israel in 1948* exhibit which was displayed at the University of Illinois at Chicago's Gallery 400 (Gheith 2004). The likely Palestinian expert on the matter, Dr. Walid Khalidi, general secretary of the Institute for Palestine Studies and Fellow of the American Academy of Arts and Sciences, states that 418 villages were affected (W. Khalidi 2001).

As with the other so called facts, claims of genocide by propaganda outfits and individual propagandists, such as highlighted in *EI*, are a waste of time and effort except for the immoral damage they do to their "enemy," believed only through ignorance or desire to believe anything bad printed about Israel.

# Chapter Ten

# The 2013 Kuala Lumpur War Crimes Tribunal Redux

Francis A Boyle, attorney and professor of international law at the University of Illinois, served as a prosecutor at the 2013 Kuala Lumpur Tribunal wherein he accused Israel of committing genocide against the Palestinian people, starting in 1948 and continuing through today. His final instruction to the judges; "Shake up the entire world! Get humanity to act to save Palestine and the Palestinians from further annihilation and genocide by Israel! Make sure that Palestine and the Palestinians are still alive twenty years from now! Convict Israel for genocide!" (Boyle 2013). Of course, no reasonable human being can actually believe that a people who have increased their population from 1.4 million to 12 million in 68 years is in any danger of disappearing in the next twenty years. Indeed, most projections show a growth in the Arab Palestinian population that will likely see their numbers exceed 25 million in 20 years. Obviously, Boyle's theatrical fears are unfounded.

During his argument, Boyle stated that when referring to the 2008-2009 Israeli excursion into Gaza, "Operation Cast Lead," U.N. General Assembly President Miguel d'Escoto Brockmann "condemned it as 'genocide'" (Boyle 2013). Boyle's reference, an article from Al-Jazeera which proclaims genocide in the headline, indicates that President Brockman never mentioned the word genocide. In fact, as reported by Al-Jazeera, Brockmann said the violence was "untenable" (Al-Jazeera 2009). Again,

Boyle's linguistic road, transforming untenable, which means "unable to defend," into genocide, is potholed beyond belief.

During the trial, Boyle claimed that he "won a so-called Article 74(4) World Court Order for Bosnia against Yugoslavia for genocide" (Boyle 2013). Of course, as the world knows, the former Yugoslavia (Serbia) was cleared of all responsibility for the genocide, other than the charge that it did not do enough to stop the genocide. Not only that, but Boyle's World Court order did not even stop the murderous ethnic cleansing in Bosnia. The "provisional measure of protection" (Boyle 2003, 160) that Boyle claims he won was in fact a meaningless piece of paper that protected nothing and protected no one. In fact, the only sustained charge of genocide in the Bosnian conflict dealt with the Bosnian Serb slaughter of approximately 8,000 Bosniak prisoners in 3 days in Srebrenica, a fact that Boyle failed to mention. Of course, Boyle also failed to mention that the court ruled against Bosnia concerning any reparations being due from the former Yugoslavia in that the "failure to prevent" conviction did not call for reparation as remedy.

Finally, referring to Ilan Pappé's *Ethnic Cleansing of Palestine*, Boyle states "As Pappé's analysis established, Zionism's 'final solution' to Israel's much-touted and racist 'demographic threat' allegedly posed by the very existence of the Palestinians has always been genocide...." (Boyle 2013), except Pappé himself denies that the Arab exodus from British Mandate Palestine was genocide.

Unfortunately, this is not the first time Boyle has railed against Israel while throwing about charges of genocide.

### Palestine: Sue Israel for Genocide before the International Court of Justice!

In 2000, Boyle wrote a paper encouraging the Palestinian Authority to institute legal proceedings against Israel, stating:

> "I am sure we can all agree that Israel has indeed perpetrated the international crime of genocide against the

Palestinian people. The purpose of this lawsuit would be to demonstrate that undeniable fact to the entire world. These world court proceedings will prove to the entire world that and to all of history that what the Nazis did to the Jews a generation ago is legally similar to what the Israelis are currently doing to the Palestinians today: genocide." (Boyle 2000, 161)

Of course, Boyle's accusations are generalizations and he does not give any specifics as to how the comparatively small loss of life, as well as the enormous population growth of the Palestinian people, gives credibility to any charge of genocide. But it does not appear that Boyle's main concern is the alleviation of Palestinian suffering. Indeed, based on his 2000 paper, it seems that Boyle is profoundly interested in punishing both Israel and the United States, perhaps going so far as to hope for their destruction. After all, in his conclusion, Boyle states that if the Palestinian suit is even filed, the result will be:

> "a severe defeat for Israel in the court of world opinion. ... [It] would deliver yet another body blow to Israel along the same lines as the major body-blow already inflicted on Israel by the creation of the State of Palestine in 1988. Israel has *never* recovered from the creation of the Palestinian State. So too, Israel will *never* recover from this genocide lawsuit brought against it by Palestine before the International Court of Justice. Likewise, the United States government will *never* recover from a World Court lawsuit brought against it by Palestine for aiding and abetting Israeli genocide against the Palestinian people."
> (Boyle 2000, 166)

Never recover? Boyle does not go on to explain what "never recover" actually means, and as Arafat's declaration of statehood in 1988 was a rather meaningless affair, it follows that Boyle's discourse is the same as Martin Shaw's opinion of Ahmadinejad's rhetoric – "wild" (Shaw 2013, 7).

Unfortunately, Boyle did not stop there. He has "repeatedly asked for his (Arafat) permission to file this lawsuit for genocide against Israel on behalf of Palestine and the Palestinian people" to no avail (Boyle, 2002). Indeed, in his 2003 book, *Palestine, Palestinians, & International Law*, Boyle mentions genocide several times, all of them as accusations that Israel is planning genocide and/or Israel is committing genocide:

1. "Heralding the onset of intensifying repression against Palestinians in occupied Palestine, possibly to the point of genocide (Boyle 2003, 47),"
2. "A Palestinian civil war and self-extermination is precisely what the Israelis have in mind for you. This is the Israeli 'Final Solution'..." (Boyle 2003, 100),
3. "I submit that if something is not done quite soon by the American people and the international community to stop Israeli war crimes and crimes against humanity being perpetrated against the Palestinian people on an ongoing basis, it could very well degenerate into genocide, if the situation has not deteriorated to that point already" (Boyle 2013, 129),
4. "Palestine has a valid claim that Israel and its predecessors-in-law – numerous Zionist agencies, forces, and terrorist gangs – have actively committed genocide against the Palestinian people that started on or about 1948 and has continued apace until today in violation of the Genocide convention..." (Boyle 2003, 159),
5. "Today, over 132 states are contracting parties to the Genocide Convention. We must pressure all of them to have the courage, integrity, and principles to sue Israel at the World Court in order to stop its ongoing and longstanding campaign of genocide against the Palestinians (Boyle 2003, 160)," and
6. "Apply[ing] the 1973 Apartheid Convention to dismantle Israel's genocidal apartheid regime" (Boyle 2003, 161).

It seems fitting to end this chapter with one last ridiculous quote from Boyle. From his 52-page pamphlet, "The Palestinian Right of Return under International Law," Boyle states:

> 'Israel' has never been anything but a Bantustan for Jews set up in the Middle East after the Second World War by the genocidal racist Western colonial/imperial who wished to severely limit the inflow of Jewish war refugees into their own states. Their intent was rather to force them to serve as Western imperialism's attack dog and genocidal enforcer against the Arab and Muslim world.... (Boyle 2011, 52)

How anyone expects to be taken seriously as a scholar or an attorney after making statements like the above is anyone's guess. However, it reiterates Deborah Lipstadt's statement, in chapter two, that a professor's responsibility, as in the case of Francis A. Boyle, "to maintain some fidelity to the notion of truth," has been removed.

# Chapter Eleven

# A Different Roadmap

Clare Brandabur, a professor of English whose specialty is comparative literature, is a different type of genocide accuser. In 2008, she wrote a 12 page paper called "Roadmap to Genocide" wherein she claims that "Israel intended ultimately to drive out and/or exterminate the indigenous people" (Brandabur 2008, 25). Of course, the act of exterminating, any people, regardless if they are indigenous or not, is genocide. However, she offers no proof of this intention.

What differs Brandabur from most genocide accusers is that she compares the Israeli treatment of the Palestinians to the treatment of the Native Americans, "whole tribes driven farther and farther away from their original habitat, deprived of their use of the land, corralled into ever smaller and more remote 'Reservations,' starved, hunted down, and finally exterminated" (Brandabur 2008, 25).

Of course, the Native Americans were driven upwards of a thousand and more miles from their home grounds and they were certainly deprived of sustainable hunting grounds. But there is no real comparison between the treatment of native Americans and the Palestinian population transfer which was more like the common practice of the same in the 20th century (Özsu 2013), most noted in the aftermath of the pre-WWI Balkan Wars, WW I and WW II.

For the majority of Arab residents, movement meant relocation to another part of British Mandate Palestine or across the River Jordan into other areas of historic Palestine (historic Palestine, contrary to Palestinians who only refer to British Mandate Palestine as "Historic Palestine," contains thousands of square miles on the eastern bank of the Jordan River (Pro-Con, 2009, citing Gosta Ahlstrom, *The History of Ancient Palestine,* 1993)). In reality many moved only few miles away or were merely displaced from their secondary agricultural homes and forced to move back into their primary winter homes in their villages (Bard 2015).

Brandabur continues, reporting, in her own words, "numbing statistics;" that between 2000, the start of the second intifada, and 2006, 4464 Palestinians have been killed (Brandabur 2008, 26). The typical disclaimer that every life is precious and every death a tragedy notwithstanding, this is an average of 720 fatalities a year or two fatalities a day during an active war. In contrast, please look at these truly "numbing statistics:" The Lebanese murdered upwards of 3,500 Palestinians in two days at Sabra and Shatila; the Serbians murdered upwards of 8,000 Bosniaks in three days in Srebrenica; during the Anfal, Iraq murdered upwards of 182,000 Kurds in a six-month period of time. Compared to those events, there is nothing numbing about the casualties incurred by the Palestinians during the second intifada.

Brandabur next step is to claim that the second intifada was started by Ariel Sharon's "highly provocative visit to the Haram al-Sharif accompanied by some 5000 riot-helmeted Israeli police" (Brandabur 2008, 26). Of course, Sharon's visit was coordinated with Palestinian authorities (Balaban 2005, 245) and there were only 1000 police (Times 2000), but this is the least of Brandabur's unsupported accusations and faulty reporting of "facts." Professor Alan Dowdy of Notre Dame, with citations ranging from Marwan Barghouti to Ehud Ya'ari, proved that the second intifada was a reaction of the Palestinians to the "bankruptcy of the negotiating process and the full rejection of the overall Israeli conduct," and that Sharon's visit was merely a "convenient excuse"(Dowty 2005, 156).

As with many others who accuse Israel of committing genocide, Brandabur's need to redefine genocide, so that the definition would fit her "facts," brought her back to Lemkin's original papers and his struggle to refine his own concept of the word. However, as previously noted, the world defines genocide in accordance with the 1946 UNGA resolution defining genocide, the Genocide Convention, and the example of such provided by the Armenian Genocide, the Holocaust, the Rwandan Genocide, and the Cambodian Genocide; the swift murder of massive numbers of people over a short period of time with the victims only true crime being their very existence. The attempt to redefine the horror of genocide to include the forced change of a national pattern of culture, in a particular place, is almost obscene. In essence, Lemkin gave up control of the definition of the word genocide in return for the UN resolution establishing the Genocide Convention.

Of course, Brandabur's paper could be excused as just another piece of propaganda meant to stir up the undereducated and the willfully ignorant. After all, she does use the stock pejorative phrases meant to inspire negative feelings towards Israel; the liberal use of such terms as genocide, ethnic cleansing, apartheid, and phrases such as "barbarous practices," "justify every barbarism required," and references to "Zionism [being the] new religion of American Jews" and "Israel their new God," are certainly meant to provoke feeling of hatred. Further, she repeats old canards such as the one about pregnant Palestinian women being deliberately kept at checkpoints until they give birth, the better chance of both dying, and the manic devotion to ethnic exclusivity taking precedence over all ethical consideration, which brings to mind the German Nazi's devotion to the extermination of the Jews taking precedence over winning World War II. This being the perverse notion of winning the peace, having a *Judenrein* (Jew free) Europe, while losing the war.

Utilization of the works of disgraced academics, such as Ward Churchill and Norman Finkelstein, round out the picture as to what lengths Brandabur will go to try prove her unprovable points. For some reason, Brandabur brings in Katz's exclusionary theory as to genocide being only applicable to the Holocaust and then uses Churchill to disprove it. However, other than Katz, there are next to no current noted genocide scholars who subscribe to his exclusionist theory. Brandabur continues with other theories including ones that infer that settler-colonial projects are inherently genocidal, an act of "Social Darwinism" in that there is a contest as to who is fittest, instigated by the party (Israel) that believes it is the fittest.

The Palestinian prison population is another sore spot for Brandabur. She states that 9,000 and 12,000 Arab prisoners are being held by Israel while also accusing Israel of holding uncounted numbers of Palestinians in secret prisons. The earlier figure is about 0.25% of the Palestinian population (Brandabur 2008, 36). And this is a population that is still in a state of war with Israel. Why she cannot seem to recall her source for this information is not puzzling. It is almost routine for Brandabur to leave off citations when it is obvious that she is exaggerating. Setting the record straight, the BBC stated that "(a)ccording to Israeli, Palestinian and human rights groups' figures, there are somewhere between 7,000 and 8,500 Palestinians held for security reasons in Israel" (BBC 2009) and at the end of 2008, B'Tselem's, a "neutral to anti-Israeli government" human rights NGO based in Israel, reported 6,500 Palestinians being held (D. J. Kramer 2012, 2178).

Regardless, Israel ranks 53 out of 222 states in the percentage of population in prison, so considering the situation, the numbers are quite normal (ICPS n.d.). Brandabur's additional comparison of the Israeli prison situation to the British "pipeline" in Kenya, the notorious Holu prison wherein 11 inmates were clubbed to death for refusal to cooperate in 1959 during the Mau Mau uprising, is outlandish (Brandabur 2008, 36) (Biles 2012).

However, Brandabur is not content with the outlandish. She quickly goes to the bizarre in writing that,

> "(O)ne of the primary purposes of the First Gulf War (that of Bush Sr.(sic)) was to ethnically cleanse the thousands of guest Palestinian workers from the Gulf, though it was Palestinian labor and expertise that built and enriched the Gulf. These workers provided support for their families in the Occupied Territories, thus enabling their families to

survive the austerities of the occupation. Consequently, under US auspices, Kuwait set up centers for interrogation and torture of Palestinians, over-seen by American officers, and Palestinians lost their residence permits and were forced to leave." (Brandabur 2008, 38).

Of course, Brandabur provides no citation for this absurdity.

Another bit of information that is without citation deals with the goal of the Israeli government. Brandabur claims that, with a maniacal devotion to maintaining an exclusively Jewish state, successive Israeli governments have "admitted" that this goal "takes precedence over all ethical considerations" (Brandabur 2008, 27). Further, there is a quote Brandabur attributes to Ariel Sharon regarding the invasion of Lebanon in 1982. She tells us Sharon said it was necessary to "to stop the rockets from raining down on the northern settlements." However, a search of the Internet only turns up Brandabur's 2008 paper as the source of this quote. She follows that up writing that the "1982 invasion was designed to… exterminate as many Palestinians in the Lebanese refugee camps as possible…" There are no citations, of course, as there are no sources for any of this propaganda.

Brandabur continues with a false litany of genocide accusations. She describes an interview with noted "new" historian, Benny Morris, wherein he complains that the state should have totally removed the Arab population from its borders, as Israeli policy. How Morris' complaint becomes the official and secret Israel state policy is a mystery. Brandabur also mentions writers who describe the Israeli genocide while neglecting to state anything about genocide. These writers include Edward Said (Brandabur 2008, 30), and Sarah Roy (Brandabur 2008, 35).

Brandabur finally wraps up her accusations with a gauntlet of propaganda from such sources as:

1.  Bamford who charges that the USS Liberty was attacked to hide the use of napalm against civilians and other genocidal crimes,

2.  Nur Masalha who states that there is an Israeli planned destruction of the Al-Aqsa Mosque and Dome of the Rock on the Temple Mount,

3.  A "Final Solution" to the Palestinian Problem, the war against Iraq is to be used as cover to remove 2 million Arabs from Israel, as well as other conspiracy theories so ridiculous as to lose Brandabur any vestige of credibility she might have had, especially as her source (Masalha) admitted that his source (*Moledet*) often carries "disinformation articles" (Brandabur 2008, 43-44).

# Chapter Twelve

# Israel's Willing Accomplices

Before delving into the accusations of Professor James Petras' that Israel is a genocidal state, it seems best to take a turn into the 2008 sideshow of dueling letters in the New York Times between Petras and Professor Benny Morris, professor of history in the Middle East Studies department of Ben-Gurion University. This duel began with Morris' July 18, 2008 Op-Ed recommending a conventional attack on Iran's nuclear sites for the purpose of destroying Iran's nuclear weapons production capability. Morris' main point being that failing such destruction, nuclear war is likely a distinct possibility, once Iran acquires a nuclear weapon (Morris 2008a).

Professor Petras, the retired Bartle Professor of Sociology at Binghamton University, responding in a July 30 letter to the Times, accusing Morris of advocating, not the destruction of nuclear facilities, but total destruction of Iran through nuclear bombardment, with a resulting death toll of 70 million. As the New York Times Letters-to-the-Editor section is not edited for veracity, and as freedom of speech, no matter how fallacious, is typically sacred in the United States, the Times let Petras rant, incredulously, for 10 paragraphs with an unsupported diatribe accusing a large number of Jewish organizations, US government offices, and the New York Times of aiding and abetting this call for nuclear genocide. In between these invectives, Petras added terms and phrases such as "Ziofascism," "Israeli genocide-ethnocide advocate," "Morris' totalitarian views," "Morris' lunacy," "Morris' totalitarian genocidal policies," "Morris' criminal advocacy of Zionist nuclear terror," "the Israeli counterpart of

Hitler's gas chambers and ovens," "Extermination is the last stage of Zionism," and finally, "That Morris is utterly, starkly and clinically insane is beyond question" (Petras 2008a).

As can be expected, Morris replied with a short retort denying Petras' charges and questioning Petras' qualifications to make any charge at all, based on the number of factual inaccuracies in Petras' letter (Morris 2008b). Not be outdone, or out-belittled, Petras' replied on August 6th, writing an article this time, continuing in the same format but with some new invectives: "Zionist genocide promoter, Benny Morris practices the Big Lie," and "Morris' promotion of Judeo-fascist ethnocide" (Petras 2008b). While one can state with absolute certainty that Petras is anti-Israel, it appears that Petras certainly crosses the line into antisemitism.

With this information in mind, reviewing Petras three articles concerning genocide requires shining a different critical light. In 2002, Petras wrote an article wherein he defended the Nobel Prize (literature) winning author, Jose Saramago, against criticism that arose from Saramago's comparison of Ramallah to Auschwitz. Starting with a fantasy of horror, Petras misquotes Saramago and then discusses the resulting furor from the Israeli public and other notables (Petras 2002). Of course, that was not all Saramago stated or did not state. Indeed, in a visit to Ramallah that occurred shortly after the Passover 2002 suicide bombing at the Park Hotel in Netanya, Israel that killed 30 people and wounded 140 more, Saramago expressed no grief for these murdered innocents. Instead, he toured areas damaged during fighting between Israeli and Palestinian armed forces and pronounced to a Portuguese radio interviewer: "[I]n Palestine, there is a crime which we can stop. We may compare it with what happened at Auschwitz" (Bancroft-Hinchey, 2002).

Both Goldhagen (*The Devil that Never Dies*) and Chesler (*The New Anti-Semitism*) condemned Saramago's antisemitism stemming from this article published in a Spanish newspaper:

> "[C]ontaminated by the monstrous and rooted 'certitude'
> that in this catastrophic and absurd world there exists

a people chosen by God ... the Jews endlessly scratch their own wound to keep it bleeding, to make it incurable, and they show it to the world as if it were a banner. Israel seizes hold of the terrible words of God in Deuteronomy: 'Vengeance is mine, and I will be repaid.'" (Goldhagen, 2013)

Petras major offence is his antisemitic criticism of Israeli policy, comparing Israel's defense of its citizens to Nazi Germany's conduct during the Holocaust. As told many times before, comparing Israel to Nazi Germany is little more than a gratuitous backhanded slap, as reflected in an article written by The Economist blogger, Blighty:

The Jews who were murdered in the Holocaust could not be responsible for any of Israel's policies, since they died before Israel existed. Israel and the Jews are related but separate entities: one is a modern state, which since its relatively recent birth has had governments of various ideological complexions; the other are a people with a much longer history, who reside in many countries across the world. Introducing the Nazis and the Holocaust into arguments about Israel, especially as a reproach, conflates the two concepts. And this conflation, which in short order blames all Jews for the actions of a state to which many owe no allegiance, is the high road to anti-Semitism.

Second, the comparison is absurd. Israel has made many mistakes in its relations with the Palestinians, and committed many offences; it has caused unjustified suffering among innocent civilians. (Sadly it may be about to cause more, albeit in response to grave provocation.) But it has done all this in the context of a political and territorial conflict. The Nazi Holocaust was an act of genocide that killed 6m Jews, motivated by annihilationist ethnic hatred.

In scale and purpose the two cases are so different that to compare them is preposterous. To say that they are alike "except for the mass murder", as some people do, is the same as saying that they are not alike.

Worse than preposterous, the comparison is offensive— and in some cases, I think, intentionally offensive. Indeed, since the Nazi reference is useless as a tool of analysis, sometimes its only point seems to be to offend. (Blighty 2014)

In 2003, Professor James Petras wrote "War & Premeditated Genocide" in which he claims that the U.S. has planned genocide in Iraq as the Nazis planned the Final Solution at the Wannsee Conference. Of course, for whatever reason, Petras quickly discloses that several of the planners are Jewish. Petras claims the main goal of the "genociders" is:

"They want genocide now: they are obsessed that all of their planning, their fantasies of world power and a Middle-East under Anglo-Israeli control, free of Arab resistance will go naught – that they personally will fail and go down in history as the genociders who were defeated by their own people." (Petras 2003)

Background aside, in 2014, as a response to the latest installment of the Israeli-Gaza War, in which the now pale and weak Palestinian Goliath, a mere shadow of his former self, once again had his dreams of glory turned into nightmares by the exuberant Israeli David, Petras sought to denigrate Israel with charges of genocide. Of course, the first step in that process is to pull the holocaust chestnuts out of the fire: "This was a sickening reminder of the Nazi roundup of Polish Jews herding them into the Warsaw Ghetto," "In line with this super race mythology, Israel's killing machine is really most effective at murdering unarmed civilians," "Informed Israeli Jews... wear their endorsement of the Gaza Holocaust as a badge of honor," and "This mirrored the Nazi policy toward those trapped in the Warsaw Ghetto" (Petras 2014).

Petras attempts to tie all Zionist organizations throughout the world together with "Israel's political elite, military command, and the mass of the Israeli public" as actively committing genocide as well as profiting from genocide. He states that "ideological affinities and ethno-religious loyalties aside, many Israeli Jews also have a major, material stake in robbing and expelling the people of Palestine… Pillage forms an important material basis for Israel's high standard of living." Finally, Petras goes all the way down the road, accusing Israel of planning world domination – "Greater Israel is no longer the crackpot dream of Jewish visionaries; it is underway and its bloody beginnings in Gaza foreshadow bigger and bloodier wars against humanity in the future" (Petras 2014).

It should seem clear that Petras is one of the genocide accusers who have flights of fancy, or as Benny Morris states, "This is all nonsense, a figment of Petras' febrile imagination. How do 'professors' invent such nonsense?" (Morris 2008).

Ramona Wadi, writing in Mint Press News, an alternative online newspaper, accuses the UN of being Israel's willing accomplice (Wadi 2014). Of course, as often noted with writers who accuse Israel of committing genocide, Wadi starts by fabricating statistics. She claims that of the approximately 2000 killed (apparently all by Israel) the majority were women and children. Of course, the statistics from Palestinian sources, reported by the UN, state that of 2104 Palestinians who died in the conflict, 495 were children (under age 18) and 253 were women (Booth 2014). That includes those who died from Hamas rockets falling back into populated areas of Gaza. Regardless of responsibility, the vast majority of those who died during the conflict were men over the age of 18. It is unknown how many counted as children were actually Hamas militants between the ages of 15 and 17.

Wadi continues her accusation by singling out Israeli leaders. Her first *J'acusse* is directed toward Ayelet Shaked, an Israeli minister. Shaked is accused of stating that all Palestinian mothers should be killed. In actuality, Shaked's stated desire is the deaths of those Palestinian mothers who encourage and praise their children's martyrdom through terrorism. "Now this also includes the mothers of the martyrs, who send them to hell with flowers and kisses. They should follow their sons, nothing would be more just" (Tharoor 2015). While nothing to admire, Shaked's call is a far cry from genocide and it certainly does not call for the death of all Palestinian mothers.

Next on Wadi's hit list is Israeli Knesset member Feiglin, who calls for moving the population of Gaza to the Sinai Peninsula to await relevant emigration destinations (Feiglin 2014). Wadi turns this around and states that Feiglin real goal is "exterminating the indigenous Palestinian population" (Wadi 2014).

Wadi's third and final "villain" is Major General Giora Eiland, who states that Israel should go to war with the state of Gaza. Aside from being upset that Eiland referred to Gaza as a state, rather than part of the still non-existent state of Palestine, Wadi is angry because Eiland states that because the residents of Gaza freely elected a genocidal regime into power, they are also to blame for the violence, just as were the German people who elected the Nazis into the German government.

Equating Gaza with Nazi Germany is more than Wadi can bear. To her, this is "marketing the Holocaust memory as an allegedly rational excuse for exterminating the Palestinian population" (Wadi 2014). Tying in with this notion is Wadi's diatribe against the UN which she states "restrict(s) the interpretation of genocide to one that encompasses the Holocaust and its guilt industry, in order to prevent a wider interpretation that should also encompass Israel's genocide against Palestinians in Gaza" (Wadi 2014).

As Benny Morris might say: How do "journalists" invent such nonsense?

# Chapter Thirteen

# Various State and World Leaders

When a state or regional power leader, whether elected, appointed (by themselves or an inside power), or inherited, takes the stage to condemn Israel, it is typically a political attack; long on form and short on fact. The cries of genocide emanating from these leaders who routinely speak of such matters are as likely to be as hypocritical as they are fallacious.

The president of Turkey, Tayyip Erdogan, made such a statement in July of 2014. However, his accusation was made with a religious overtone to make the accusation sound much worse in the ears of Muslims. Erdogan stated, "Since (the creation of the state of Israel) in 1948 we have been witnessing this attempt at systematic genocide every day and every month. But above all we are witnessing this attempt at systematic genocide every Ramadan" (AFP 2014). Of course, that is not the first time a Turkish leader has charged Israel with committing genocide. In 2002, "Turkish Prime Minister Bulent Ecevit said 'genocide' is being committed by Israeli forces in the territories" (Forward 2002). What is telling is that the charge was later recanted due to a contract Turkey procured for Israel to upgrade Turkey's battle tanks (Forward 2002).

Accusing Israel of committing genocide, so that it deliberately coincides with the Islamic observance of Ramadan, makes the supposed commission of such a heinous crime so much worse, as a Muslim is supposed to be fasting and refraining from false speech, sex, and fighting, in order to attain a greater degree of spirituality during that time. Imagine the horror of committing such a heinous crime against a people engaged in such spirituality! However, this scenario is quite hypocritical as per these examples of Muslims at war with other Islamic states; Iran attacked Iraq during Ramadan of 1982 and refused cease fires from Iraq during the Ramadan periods of 1981 and 1987, Syria and Egypt attacked Israel during Ramadan 1973, coincidentally(?) during Yom Kippur when even the least religious Israelis would likely be in a synagogue without outside world communications, the Yemenite and Lebanese Civil wars, respectively, continued through several Ramadans, and Hamas launched the missiles that started the 2014 conflict in Gaza during Ramadan, the very same Ramadan referenced by Erdogan.

Later in that same July, Erdogan accused Israel of surpassing Hitler's Holocaust in its treatment of the Palestinians in Gaza. Additionally, he stated that "Israel is not even approaching such a thing [peace] and is spitting death, spitting blood" (Zaman 2014).

Of course, Turkey has been denying its genocidal history for almost a century. There are few who do not know the genocide committed by the Ottomans from 1915 through 1923 as they tried to ethnically purify their shrinking empire by murdering the Armenians, Greeks, and Assyrians living among them, under the cover of World War I (WW I) and the subsequent regional wars.

Fidel Castro's accusations: "Fidel Castro has accused Israel of practicing 'a new, repugnant form of fascism' in its brutal war against the Gaza Strip, constituting a 'macabre genocide'" (MEMO 2014). Of course, what makes a particular genocide "macabre," and another not, is unknown.

Accusation of genocide also supposedly came from the President of the UN, Miguel d'Escoto Brockmann, in 2009 (Chomsky and Pappé 2010). Chomsky and Pappé seem to believe that Brockmann's failure to charge genocide, in actual situations wherein the charge would be accurate, to have special meaning to show how vile Israel is in its dealings with Gaza. But in actuality in merely reveals how easy it is for non-Western politicians to attack Israel. Indeed, because Israel is a western-style liberal democracy with a free press, no false accuser fears physical retaliation.

Curiously, this is the same accusation, proven false, made by Francis A. Boyle in chapter 10 of this book. Again, while many sources state that Brockmann used the word "genocide," no reliable citation shows him actually using that word.

Of course, there are few politicians who match the fiery rhetoric of Bangladeshi Jatiya Party (JP) chairman HM Ershad, who is also a special envoy to the Bangladesh Prime Minister, who not only denounced Israel as being genocidal, and not only stated that "Israel is the stigma of the world. Down with Israel and it be demolished," but also declared that "Now we can understand why Hitler had killed the Jews" (The Financial Express 2014).

Finally we come to the president of the Palestinian Authority and the Chairman of the Palestinian Liberation Organization (PLO), Mahmoud Abbas. At the UN, in the opening days of the September 2014 session, According to journalist Larry Derfner, Abbas dropped this "bombshell:"

> Mahmoud Abbas' speech last Friday at the United Nations General Assembly gave the highest-profile-ever exposure to the accusation, popular among anti-Zionists, that Israel practices "genocide" against the Palestinians, and that the war in Gaza was a genocidal one. That's the highlight of the speech that was picked for the headline in any number of major international news outlets; in Israel the speech is already known, and will be forever, as Abbas' "genocide speech." That one word seems to have overshadowed everything else he said at the UN podium....
>
> If his use of the term "genocide" to describe the occupation and the war in Gaza were truthful but "impolitic," that would be one thing. But it's not true – it's plain false. And on top of that, it's impolitic in the extreme – it's politically suicidal, precisely because it's so clearly false. It's an Achilles heel in the argument against the occupation. It allows the right wing to sweep aside everything else, in

this case every true thing that Abbas said at the UN, and zero in on that one blatant falsehood. It stamps the anti-occupation cause with fanaticism, with reckless disregard for the truth, with hysterical hatred for Israel. That one stupid word. (Derfner 2014)

Clearly when the Palestinian state leader claims that Israel is committing genocide, the only people intently listening are those who want to believe Israel committed genocide. As Derfner points out, such a charge energizes the base group of Israel haters, and may recruit a few ignorant college students to become activists, and, although he fails to mention the slight possibility, the accusation may give radical Palestinians greater justification for attacks on Israelis (Derfner 2014).

Derfner also admits that such a charge is the political equivalent of "shoot[ing] oneself in the foot, if not the head." Finally, Derfner states that:

When you accuse Israel of committing genocide against the Palestinians, you are accusing it of deliberately, systematically executing them *en masse*, hundreds of thousands or millions of them. You're accusing Israel of an attempt to exterminate an entire people, like the Nazis did the Jews, like the Ottoman Turks did the Armenians, like the Hutus did the Tutsis in Rwanda. That's what people think of when they hear the word "genocide." That was not the war in Gaza, and that's not the occupation. (Derfner 2014)

Chapter Fourteen

# Is Israel Genghis Khan with a Computer?

In 2011, Douglas Anthony Cooper, a somewhat controversial writer for the Huffington Post, took exception to Norman Finkelstein's pronouncements regarding the nature of Israel and the nature of the Israeli-Palestinian conflict. One such upsetting statement made by Finkelstein is that "Israel is Genghis Kahn with a computer" (Gutasli 2009). Other statements, which Cooper finds equally upsetting, are; "Sometimes I feel that Israel has come out of the boils of hell, a satanic state," and "Israel is committing a genocide in Gaza (Gutasli 2009). Clearly, Finkelstein has some problems with the state of Israel. Cooper, among others, has a problem with Finkelstein's opinions.

Cooper decided to conduct research in order to determine if Israel is the genocidal menace Finkelstein portends it to be. Is Israel the insane, rogue, vandal state that so many ultra-liberals and third world state leaders claim it to be? The following numbers are over five years old, as Cooper's articles were written in 2011, leaving out the data from the last two Gaza Wars which claimed about 3,500 Gazan lives, the majority from Israeli action.

Cooper used websites such as http://www.necrometrics.com, http://www.war-memorial.net/Israel-vs-Palestine-3.217, http://www.pcr.uu.se/research/ucdp/ datasets/ucdp_prio_armed_conflict_dataset/, and http://www.btselem.org/statistics for his casualty figures. For those concerned with objective sources, the last two are reputed to favor the Palestinian side. Before putting the figures down of paper, here is Cooper's caveat: "We are talking about 'human beings, each... loved and mourned.' The difference between one number and another one, number higher, is the world of difference to that person's family. The numbers are only important for comparative reasons" (Cooper 2011a).

The totality of Palestinian lives lost since 1948, by the hands of the Israelis, up through July of 2010 is less than 30,000 people, armed and unarmed, firing on Israelis or totally innocent men, women, and children as tragic collateral damage (Cooper 2011b). This includes the Nakba up through the aftermath of Protective Edge. Less than thirty thousand lives lost in the space of 63 years. Again, lest anyone makes accusations of callousness, every life is sacred and every life lost is a tragedy, but the facts speak for themselves; "relative to the world's genocides and relative to the size of the populous (the loss of life) is astonishingly low" (Cooper 2011b).

This is not Finkelstein's first or last foray on his website accusing Israel of being genocidal. There is the posting of an article written by Michael Brizon (writing as B. Michael) on Finkelstein's website wherein Brizon accuses the Israeli Agriculture Minister Yair Shamir of inciting genocide via his suggestion of requiring monogamy of the Bedouin tribes as a method of reducing the prolific birth rate. Brizon is in turn nauseated, filled with revulsion, and finally reduced to bitter laughter, but not driven to read the genocide convention to see if such actually falls under its auspices (Brizon 2014).

Brizon compares the goal and desired method of the Israeli minister in an amazing display of historical and factual ignorance. He writes, "such racist discourse has not come from any sane administration since the days of Pharaoh." Of course, the proposal from Pharaoh, made to decrease the number of Hebrews (not decrease the number of births) was "When you deliver the Hebrew women, and you see on the birth stool, if it is a son, you shall put him to death" (Exodus 1:16). Brizon's article is a typical polemical work favored by Finkelstein, which takes him out of the scholarly world and into the world of propaganda.

Luckily, the Office of the UN Special Advisor on the Prevention of Genocide (OSAPG) has provided an "official" interpretation of Article

2(d): Imposing measures intended to prevent births within the group. The OSAPG considers such to be programs intended to prevent procreation, including involuntary sterilization, forced abortion, total prohibition of marriage, and long-term separation of men and women (OSAPG 2015).

The key term in the genocide convention is "prevent birth," not reduce births. If introducing measures to cause a reduction in the birth rate were a genocidal crime, the Chinese government, who for years have had a "one child per family" law in effect, would surely be put before the International Criminal Court. However, not only has it not been referred, it has not even been a question. Requiring monogamy instead of allowing polygamy hardly prevents birth.

Finkelstein posted an AP article from 2006 which had absolutely nothing to do with genocide but dealt with the hardships facing Gaza. Finkelstein's title? – "Another day, another Genocide" (AP 2006). Finally, there is the 2010 interview he gave to Lena Meari and Tanzeen Doha, which was published in Chintaa. In that interview, Finkelstein equalized the deliberate gassing and cremating little Jewish girls by the German Nazis with the accidental burning of innocent children in the onetime Israel use of white phosphorus in an illegal manner, for the purpose of burning brush (Doha 2010). Because of this particular charge by Finkelstein, Cooper accuses Finklestein of being determined, for whatever reason, to paint Jews "as a race of eager child-killers" (Cooper 2011c.)

Cooper's investigation of Finkelstein's accusation, that Israel is "Genghis Khan with a computer," reveals much about Finkelstein's likely mental state. One does not have to be a historian to know who Genghis Khan was. He is easily recognized as one of the most, if not the most, murderous conquerors in history. Based on population differences at the time, Genghis Kahn may have killed a greater percentage of mankind than was killed during all of World War II (Andrews 2014). How does anyone have the irrational world view to compare Israel to the Mongol Horde?

Cooper explains the impossibility of the comparison by utilizing magnitudes. At its simplest, a magnitude is a power of ten; a dollar is one magnitude greater than a dime which is one magnitude greater than a penny. But those comparisons seem so small. The following is a better example to use. A man is 6 feet tall, a five stories tall building (60 ft.) is one magnitude taller, and a fifty stories tall building (600 ft.) is two magnitudes taller. A 500 story building (6000 ft), about 4 times taller than any building ever built, is only 3 magnitudes taller than a man. Genghis Khan killed upwards of 40 million people. Israel killed less than 20 thousand unarmed civilians. That is more than a three magnitude difference. It is greater than the difference in height between a man and a thousand stories tall building, about 12,000 feet, a building over 2 miles high.

# Chapter Fifteen

# Sabra and Shatila

The 1982 massacre at the Lebanese settlements, for Palestinian refugees since 1948, of Sabra and Shatila, while under occupation by Israeli forces, was likely the low point of the overall occupation of Lebanon by the Israeli Defense Force. This episode is the closest Israel has ever come to being involved in an act of genocide. As will be shown in the following paragraphs, the Israeli Special Commission set up to investigate the massacre did come to the conclusion that Israel bore indirect responsibility.

While declared a genocide by the UNGA in a resolution condemning a variety of Israeli actions, the relevant portion of the resolution did not name the Israelis as having committed genocide, just that genocide occurred. Surprisingly, the UNGA resolution (A/RES/37/123); (6) deplores Israel's failure to comply with Security Council resolutions ; (7) Condemns Israel's aggression and practices against the Palestinian People;(8) Strongly condemns the imposition by Israel of its laws, jurisdiction and administration on the occupied Syrian Golan Heights, all by name. Yet without naming a responsible party, the UNGA states in the same resolution that it; (1) Condemns in the strongest terms the large-scale massacre of Palestinian civilians in the Sabra and Shatila refugee camps; (2) Resolves that the massacre was an act of genocide (UNGA 1982). Not only did the UNGA resolution neglect to name any state or group as being responsible for the genocide, if indeed it was genocide, they also failed to recognize that Pakistanis, Lebanese, Iranians, Syrians, and Algerians were also killed, as if the only deaths that mattered were Palestinian deaths (Malone 1985, 374)(UNGA 1982).

As to the charge of genocide, the UNGA is not a body of legal or sociological experts who can make such a declaration with any kind of certainty. More than likely, the behavior of the Lebanese Phalangists during this horrible episode is the same behavior typified by the Ottomans when they massacred approximately 300,000 Armenians in 1895; the purpose was punishment, not eradication (Balakian 2003; Bloxham 2005).

In 2012, Dr. Christof Lehmann, advisor to Yasser Arafat and Nelson Mandela (4thMedia 2014), wrote that the events of 16-18 September 1982 could not have come about without the mainstream media, especially the American cinema, having contributed to the demonization and dehumanization of Arabs, in a sense robbing them of their humanity (Lehmann 2012). Fortunately for the reputation of the press and Hollywood, the massacre was carried out by Lebanese Christian Arabs primarily against other Lebanese and Palestinian Muslim Arabs. Perhaps Dr. Lehmann should have just looked in his history books, for the history of the conflict between the parties. He would have read about when the Lebanese Muslims massacred 40,000 Lebanese Christians (Maronites) in 1860 (Kiernan 2007, 397). Indeed, the derision and vilification directed at the departing members of the PLO, from the Maronites who lined the roads to joyously see them off, was a foreshadowing of what would happen to the Palestinians who remained behind (Tessler 2009).

The twenty two year history of Israel in Lebanon, from 1978 through 2000, consists of many tragic mistakes and an ultimate withdrawal under less than honorable conditions. Both the 1978 and 1982 invasions into Lebanon by Israel were for the purpose of ending the PLO's ability to attack Israel while the Lebanese Civil War was ongoing. After a cease fire in 1982, the Israeli-allied president-elect of Lebanon, Bachir Gemayel, was assassinated. Palestinians were blamed. Israel, along with their Lebanese Christian Maronite allies, the Phalangists, then occupied western Beirut.

With the pretext of routing out Palestinian fighters from the local Palestinian refugee settlements of Sabra and Shatila, the Israeli forces set up a perimeter encampment and allowed or ordered the Phalangists to remove the Palestinian militants. However, most, if not all, Palestinian militants had already left Beirut under an agreement reached between the parties which was guaranteed by the US.

The Phalangists entered Sabra and Shatila around 6 PM September 16th and departed around 8 AM September 18th; a period of about 38 hours (Malone 1985, 374). During that time frame, the Phalangists killed a truly unknown number of people, ranging from 300 to 3500 (Reese 2013) (Quigley 2005, 200) (Malone 1985, 374) residents, primarily Palestinian but also Pakistani, Lebanese, Iranian, Syrian, and Algerian (Malone 1985, 374). The wide difference in the number of casualties reported is because there is no reliable authority that can provide an accurate basis for any particular number.

The Kahan Commission of Inquiry reported a number of fatalities based on the count from the combination of reports it received, with the caveat that "It is impossible to determine precisely the number of persons who were slaughtered. The numbers cited in this regard are to a large degree tendentious and are not based on an exact count by persons whose reliability can be counted on" is 460 (JewishVirtualLibrary 1983). This combination number was derived from reports submitted by "the Lebanese Red Cross, the International Red Cross, the Lebanese Civil Defense, the medical corps of the Lebanese army, and by relatives of the victims" (JewishVirtualLibrary 1983). From those same lists, the Kahan Commission reported that:

> According to this count, the 460 victims included 109 Lebanese and 328 Palestinians, along with Iranians, Syrians and members of other nationalities. According to the itemization of the bodies in this list, the great majority of the dead were males; as for women and children, there were 8 Lebanese women and 12 Lebanese children, and 7 Palestinian women and 8 Palestinian children. Reports from Palestinian sources speak of a far greater number of persons killed, sometimes even of thousands. With respect to the number of victims, it appears that we can

rely neither on the numbers appearing in the document from Lebanese sources, nor on the numbers originating in Palestinian sources. A further difficulty in determining the number of victims stems from the fact that it is difficult to distinguish between victims of combat operations and victims of acts of slaughter. We cannot rule out the possibility that various reports included also victims of combat operations from the period antedating the assassination of Bashir. Taking into account the fact that Red Cross personnel counted no more that (sic) 328 bodies, it would appear that the number of victims of the massacre was not as high as a thousand, and certainly not thousands. (JewishVirtualLibrary 1983)

Still, the Kahan Commission accepted the larger figure, according to IDF intelligence sources, of between 700 and 800 fatalities. Which, in the Kahan Commission's words, "may well be the number most closely corresponding with reality. It is impossible to determine precisely when the acts of slaughter were perpetrated; evidently they commenced shortly after the Phalangists entered the camps and went on intermittently until close to their departure" (JewishVirtualLibrary 1983).

In the same context, Ariel Sharon justified allowing the Phalangists access to Sabra and Shatila in that he believed that there were between 2000 and to 3000 Palestinian militants still in the camps (Malone 1985, 413; Zieve 2012). Again, as with the fatalities, there is no reliable source for the number of Palestinian fighters still in the camps although Friedman reported that "the weight of the evidence suggests that the number was in the low hundreds at most" (Friedman 1982). Regardless, there is no report that Sharon's desire was anything more than the "destruction of the remaining Palestinian guerillas thought to still be in the city" (Mallison 1986, 391).

The initial reports of this particular incident created a wide spread protest of condemnation in Israel, sparking a mass rally attended by around 400,000 Israelis, approximately 10% of Israel's population (Zieve 2012). That rally, known as the "March of the 400,000," had the support of the full political spectrum:

> At the time of the massacre, Israel was fully in control of West Beirut. Therefore, when news of the horrifying three-day massacre reached the Israeli public, they wanted answers. They knew that Israel had not carried out the massacre themselves, however as the occupier, the government bore responsibility for the course of events; the people demanded an investigation into just how large that degree of responsibility was. (Zieve 2012)

The specific goal of the protest was the fulfillment of the demand for "the creation of a government commission to investigate Israel's role in the massacre" (Zieve 2012). With this unprecedented massive turnout of the Israeli citizenry in protest of its government's action, there is a definitive negation of Dr. Lehmann's claim of the dehumanization of Palestinians, for it appears that the imagined dehumanization of the Palestinians had no effect on the typical Israeli who seems to have understood the human aspect of the carnage inflicted on Palestinian civilians in the two camps.

The fallout from the protest march forced the Israeli government to institute the Kahan Commission, which produced its report on February 8, 1983. The Kahan Commission concluded:

> "that a Phalangist unit carried out and was directly responsible for the Sabra and Shatila massacre, and that no Israeli was directly responsible for the events. However, the Kahan Commission asserted that Israel had indirect responsibility for the massacre since the IDF held the area." (Zieve 2012)

The recommendations of the commission included removal of Ariel Sharon as Defense Minister and removal of various other senior officials and officers. While initially resisting implementing the recommendations, further demonstrations and incidents of violence in the demonstrations convinced Sharon to resign his post.

Complicating the Kahan Commission's work was the reluctance and outright refusal of witnesses to testify; some for fear of retribution, others for possible professional reasons, such as noted journalist Thomas Freedman's refusal to testify (Malone 1985, 379).

A report from Time magazine stated that Sharon instigated the massacre by advising the Gemayel family the "need for the Phalangists to seek revenge for the assassination of Bashir Gemayel" (Malone 1985, 374). Sharon sued Time for libel and won the case, but the story still damaged Sharon's reputation.

Several parties used this incident to charge Israel with committing genocide, even though Israel neither participated in the massacre nor ordered the carnage. The Mallisons, in an attempt to find moral fault by comparing Israel's actions with those of Nazi Germany, discussed the reasons for the Genocide Convention, stating that it came about to prevent a reoccurrence of events in WW II Europe as a result of Nazi Germany's conduct during war (Mallison 1986, 388). However, as indicated in chapter 2, the Genocide Convention was actually written to deter such practices during peace time, as the initial activity began years before WW II started in 1939. Another absurd genocide charge deals with the confinement of male combatants specifically as a means of preventing births. While the men were confined, their lack of opportunity for procreation during time of war was hardly of concern to any party to the conflict.

The 1982 event was not the last massacre to occur in the vicinity of the camps. In fact, "the Palestinian refugee camps in Lebanon have consistently been the site of uncompromising brutality" (Westmoreland 2015, 134). In 1985, the camps were hit yet again, with possibly the same number of casualties as occurred in 1982, but these were inflicted under the watchful eyes of the Syrian forces and they incurred little international comment (Westmoreland 2015, 134). For whatever reason, it appears that violence against Arabs, that can be blamed on an Israeli source, gets much more attention and notoriety than violence against Arabs from an Arab source.

According to the Mallisons, the Lebanese government initiated its own investigation of the massacre but it appeared mostly for show as there were too many embarrassing ties between the Phalangists and the government (Mallison 1986, 404).

Again, as aforementioned, the UNGA, passed resolution 37/123 in 1982, wherein Israel was condemned for numerous items; mainly the failure to heed previous resolutions, continued occupation of "the Arab and Palestinian territories," the annexation of Jerusalem, and several others. There is a mention of the genocide convention and a declaration that the massacre at Sabra and Shatila was a genocide, but no party was actually blamed for the genocide (UNGA 1982). So why even deal with invoking a genocide resolution?

William Schabas, a pre-eminent genocide scholar, in his opus "Genocide in International Law," gives his opinion of the 1982 UNGA resolution, keeping in mind that ICJ had ruled that "it is widely accepted that genocide may be found to have been where the intent is to destroy the group within a geographically limited area" (Schabas 2009, 286).

Schabas states:

> A 1982 resolution of the United Nations General Assembly declared the massacre of a few hundred victims in the Palestinian refugee camps of Sabra and Shatila, located in the suburbs of Beirut, to be an 'act of genocide.' The resolution was not unanimous, however, and a separate vote on the paragraph referring to genocide was approved by ninety-eight to nineteen, with twenty-three abstentions, on a recorded vote. Doubtless, many States used the term 'genocide' to express their outrage at the atrocity in a manner calculated to torment a State whose population had itself suffered so much as a result of the same crime. A General Assembly resolution could, in theory, be of considerable assistance in construing the scope of the words 'in whole or part', as a form of authentic interpretation or

merely an indication of *opino jur* of States (Opino juris is the second element (along with state practice) necessary to establish a legally binding custom. Opino juris denotes a subjective obligation, a sense on behalf of a state that it is bound to the law in question). Yet the circumstance surrounding the adoption of the Sabra and Shatila resolution, and the lack of unanimity, argue against drawing any meaningful conclusions. (Schabas 2009, 286).

# Chapter Sixteen

# Genocide? Really?

In 2014, The Independent, a British morning newspaper, printed a story about an advertisement placed in the New York Times by Holocaust survivors and family members of survivors. The headline read, "Holocaust survivors and their descendants accuse Israel of 'genocide.'" The subtitle read, "More than 300 Holocaust survivors and their descendants have condemned what they described as Israel's 'genocide of Palestinian people' in an advert in the New York Times" (Boren 2014). But nowhere in the article was there a reprint of the actual advert. That omission was likely by design.

When the actual advert is examined, nowhere are the words "genocide of Palestinian people," found. In fact, the only reference to genocide is this rather ambiguous declaration statement, "Genocide begins with the silence of the world" (Castle 2014). Personally, I have not found any genocides, since the beginning of the Armenian Genocide in 1914, where the international community was silent if it knew what was happening.

Although covered in Chapter Eleven, Douglas Anthony Cooper's four part essay on the impossibility that Israel committed genocide, written for the Huffington Post, deserves a little more coverage. In the 17 single-spaced pages he produced, he lashed out several times at the writers and scholars who claim Israel has committed genocide. First though, he states his belief as to what would entail a genocide of the Palestinians, which is certainly close to what is meant in the legal definition; "The genocide of the Palestinians, who number in the millions, would involve at the very least Israel's concerted effort to commit murder on an unspeakable scale." (Cooper 2011a). However, the actual scale of the number killed, in comparison with similar historical events, in Cooper's words, is "astonishingly low" and "scandalously low" (Cooper 2011a).

Cooper goes on to state that anyone who genuinely and sincerely believes Israel committed genocide is "embracing an ignorance that is inseparable from the most vulgar forms of prejudice... It is a lie" (Cooper 2011b). But Cooper does not stop there. He later states, "if you consider Israel a genocidal nation, you are either incapable of distinguishing between a pond and an ocean, or you are – more likely – a bigot" (Cooper 2011b). As for Finkelstein's comparison of Genghis Kahn to Israel, Cooper states that the comparison is "particularly obscene" (Cooper 2011c).

Norman G. Finkelstein, Ph.D., is not a stupid man. He is not an ignorant man. Yet he insists that Israel is committing genocide. But surely he knows the facts. Similarly, John Docker, Francis A Boyle, and a host of others also know the facts. Regardless of knowing the facts, they still find convoluted ways to try to prove that Israel has committed genocide. Why?

Cooper provides one possible answer:

> If you put out the lie that a nation is genocidal, you strengthen its enemies. You weaken its friends. You convince otherwise well-meaning liberals that they are allied to a monster, that they enable this monster and its genocidal machinery. Decent people do not wish to be complicit in genocide. Decent people cut off funding. (Cooper 2011d)

But that is only one answer.

Edward S. Herman and David Peterson, in their book *The Politics of Genocide* discuss the political ramifications of the accusation of genocide. It is uncanny how they accurately portray how the charges fly depending on who is the victim and who is the perpetrator.

> When we ourselves commit mass atrocity crimes, the atrocities are *Constructive*, our victims are *unworthy* of

our attention and indignation, and never suffer "genocide" at our hands.... But when the perpetrator of mass-atrocity crimes is our enemy or a state targeted by us for destabilization and attack, the converse is true. Then the atrocities are *Nefarious* and their victims worthy of our focus, sympathy, public displays of solidarity. And calls for inquiry and punishment. Nefarious atrocities even have their own proper names reserved for them, typically associated with the places where the events occurred. (Herman and Peterson 2011, 103)

Of course, Herman and Peterson were referring to the United States as their "we," but "we" could just as easily stand for Turkey, China, Russia, or any number of regional powers who routinely commit crimes against humanity in sufficient numbers as to warrant investigation by the ICC. Indeed, Turkey, who committed the first genocide of the 20th century not associated with colonization, the Armenian Genocide, refuses to acknowledge that it occurred, yet charges Israel with committing genocide during the 2014 Israeli/Gaza war, and actually accuses Israel of committing "systematic genocide every Ramadan since 1948" (Sharkov 2014).

All of this simply boils down to a propaganda campaign, however uncoordinated and unconnected, to delegitimize the state of Israel. Kofi Annan, former UN General Secretary, diplomatically apologized for the rash of antisemitic and anti-Israel behavior that has plagued the UN almost from its beginnings. First, Kofi discussed the 1975 UNGA resolution that singled out Zionism as the only national movement that was racist. This ignoble resolution passed while South Africa was still fully under the control of an Apartheid regime. But Annan's "Let us acknowledge that the United Nations' record on anti-Semitism has at times fallen short of our ideals" (Annan 2004), falls short of describing the UN's near total animosity toward Israel.

The UN established a human rights organization as part of its administrative hierarchy. That institution, the UN Commission on Human Rights, was disbanded in 2006. As Professor Rosa Freedman of the University of Birmingham School of Law reports:

> Contrary to the idealistic promises of international human rights, protecting and promoting human rights at the universal level is often a zero-sum game. Time and resources are limited and choices must be made about allocating them in an even-handed manner. Attention to one problem inevitably means time or resources diverted from another. Human rights mechanisms that devote vastly disproportionate attention to gross and systemic violations within one country often fail adequately to protect and promote rights within other, similar situations. Lack of even-handedness usually results from states and groups using human rights bodies to pursue national or regional interests. Politicisation (sic) can undermine the work of international bodies, sometimes subsuming an institution to the extent that it becomes unable to fulfil its mandate.
>
> The United Nations Commission on Human Rights (UNCHR) was disbanded in 2006. The demise of the UNCHR was due largely to the selectivity, bias, and partiality that increasingly dominated its proceedings. As a result of that politicization (sic), the Commission failed to address many gross and systemic country-specific human rights violations, whilst simultaneously devoting vastly disproportionate attention to other situations. For example, during the Commission's sixty years, one quarter of its country-specific resolutions focused on Israel while not one resolution dealt with human rights abuses in China. (Freedman 2012)

The successor organization, the UN Human Rights Council (UNHRC), has not fared any better. In the ten years of its existence, with thousands murdered in Egypt, Iraq, Ukraine, and Russia (Chechnya), the UNHRC saw fit to issue 61 resolutions condemning Israel and none against the aforementioned states. Indeed, Israel received more condemnations that the rest of the world combined over that ten year period of time (Thiessen 2015)

The UN has been the sponsor of conferences that appear designed to demonize Israel. A case in point are the UN World Conferences against Racism, Racial Discrimination, Xenophobia and Related Intolerance, better known as the Durban Conferences, as the first was held in Durban, South Africa in 2001. The Conference quickly degenerated into an anti-Israeli hate-fest marked with antisemitic imagery and demagoguery. The United States, as well as Israel, withdrew from the conference by the fourth day.

One of the civic group conferences discussed removing language that would specifically condemn antisemitism. After the Jewish groups left in protest, the conference then voted to condemn Israel for ethnic cleansing and genocide (Swarns 2001). In his report regarding the withdrawal of American representation, Secretary of State Colin Powell, stated:

> "Today I have instructed our representatives at the World Conference Against Racism to return home. I have taken this decision with regret, because of the importance of the international fight against racism and the contribution that the Conference could have made to it. But, following discussions today by our team in Durban and others who are working for a successful conference, I am convinced that will not be possible. I know that you do not combat racism by conferences that produce declarations containing hateful language, some of which is a throwback to the days of "Zionism equals racism;" or supports the idea that we have made too much of the Holocaust; or suggests that apartheid exists in Israel; or that singles out only one country in the world--Israel--for censure and abuse." (Powell 2001)

The Congressional Research Service (CRS) reviewed the 2001 Durban Conference papers in order to determine if it would be appropriate for the US to participate in Durban II, the 2009 Conference. The CRS reported that previous UNGA inappropriate decisions, such as the infamous 1975 resolution declaring Zionism to be racist, received US condemnation to the extent of accusing UN member states of "treat(ing) racism not as a serious injustice, but as an 'epithet to be flung at whoever [sic] happens to be one's adversary'" (Blanchfield 2008, 4). While the CRS found that the Durban I Declaration was not as inflammatory as many of the other sessions in the Conference, it did find that Israel was the only state required by the Declaration to perform any actions.

In step with the Durban I Conference, an NGO Forum was held. However, the declaration issued by the NGO Forum was considered by many to be "an unbalanced document that disproportionately focused on Israel" (Blanchfield 2008, 13). "The U.N. High Commissioner for Human Rights Mary Robinson described the NGO Forum as 'hateful, even racist,' and refused to receive or endorse the NGO Declaration" (Blanchfield 2008, 13-14). Indeed, the NGO Forum Declaration falsely accused Israel of committing genocide several times as seen in articles 99, 160, 420, and 426 (Forum 2001).

# Chapter Seventeen

# Conclusion

All through the preceding chapters, you have read about the false accusations of genocide that are the result of international and domestic political shenanigans. In the meantime, real genocide, and conflicts that are theorized as precursors to genocide, continue elsewhere.

Steven Carter relates the proscription of the Genocide Convention in that it requires UN action, that it requires UN intervention (Carter 2011, 128). However, it appears that no regional power takes such a notion seriously. Carter states that this is merely a matter of politics. "Nations with the power to intervene do not want to intervene" (Carter 2011, 128). Indeed, "the United States has never intervened to end genocide" (Carter 2011, 132). In an illustration as to the dangers of intervention, Carter analogizes Clint Eastwood's *Unforgiven*, a morality tale wherein a victim hires an Avenger to exact vengeance, the victim's concept of justice, because she was treated unjustly. In Carter's analysis, the Avenger does more harm than good, that he does far more than what is asked. The Avenger does this to fulfill his own agenda, and that the act of vengeance itself increases the desire for violence on all sides of the conflict.

However, I believe Carter is wrong. In fact, it appears that Carter has a superficial view of the movie. In actuality, those that deserved the most punishment, the oppressive politicians, are not those who committed the crimes for which the Avenger was brought in to avenge. The politicians deserving punishment were those who meted out their version of justice, which gave the direct victim nothing and gave the indirect victim, who was going to suffer a slight economic setback for no longer having the full chargeable services of the victim, everything. All this because the indirect victim was a major power requiring mollification. And the actual victim was powerless.

This act of injustice so incenses the friends of the victim that they desire a violent act of revenge; the death of the ones that committed the physical crime, even though that crime did not merit the death penalty. It was the realization of being considered worthless, the humiliation they suffered by being treated as chattel, rather than as human beings, that drove them to seek an alternative untenable justice. Incredulously, the direct victim and her friends never thought to seek punishment against the major powers, the true source of the injustice, perhaps thinking them to be too powerful for the victim to even consider punishing.

The Avenger kills the two that committed the initial wrong. These deaths so infuriate the politicians that they seek justice on their terms; for they are now furiously and righteously indignant. But they seek justice in the only way they know how, with an overwhelming display of power. This brutality is considered moral behavior within their own system of ethics. They whip one of the Avenger's associates to death. Regardless, the Avenger is too powerful to stop.

At the beginning of the Avenger's final rampage, he stops to consider an indignant, righteous complaint; that he just shot a member of the political elite who did not carry a weapon. The Avenger retorts that one who commits such evil deeds should have the sense to be armed, as such evil cannot go unchallenged. But this is situational morality, as the Avenger is just as evil, with only age and experience tempering his soul. However, this is not a book about intervention, it is about Israel and the accusation that the state is genocidal.

There is another movie analogy that fits; M. Night Shyamalan's *Lady in the Water*. Each of the characters in the story is designated to perform a specific function and they are assigned that function by the main character utilizing what seems to be common sense, basing his decision on the particular character's physical appearance. But looks are deceiving and it turns out that the assignments are wrong. The tasks must be assigned based on the person's merits. But that is a movie and suspension of disbelief is the key concept in that movie, as well as most movies.

There is an old saying; Common sense is not common. Indeed, common sense is a projection of one's own hind-sighted thoughts onto a situation new to another. It rarely works. Both concepts, poor common sense and suspension of disbelief, fuel and guide the work of the Weirs, Boyles, Falks, Dockers, Waters, Pappés, Atzmons, and many others who either state or promote the concept that Israel has committed genocide. If only they can make the public suspend their disbelief, they will be able to convince that public that Israel deserves to be punished for a crime they have not even contemplated, let alone remotely come close to committing. And it is in that same light that enables Rashed and Short to declare that crying genocide has become a "condemnatory label of rhetorical utility," removing it far from its use as an identifier of the worst of crimes, and making it become merely the worst of accusations (Rashed and Short 2012, 1142).

Stephen Carter continues his discussion of morality in battle, dealing with those endowing the Geneva Convention "with a talismanic quality, a suggestion that by violating them, or even interpreting them loosely rather than strictly, you accept moral doom upon the entire project of your nation, now and forever." He aptly follows that with the warning that if that is your thought process and your mindset, you missed maturity (Carter 2011, 103).

Israel's President, Reuven Rivlin, addressing the UNGA, stated:

> The international community that is joined together in this organization bears the duty to lay down the red lines that define genocide - and to agree that the crossing of those red lines makes it compulsory to intervene. On the other hand, and in the same breath, we must remember that definition of the red lines requires putting an end to the devaluation and the cynical, supposedly objective usage in rhetoric on human rights of concepts such as 'genocide', for political purposes.

Thus, for years, this Assembly (whose resolution validated the establishment of the State of Israel) identified Zionism - the Jewish revival movement - with its greatest enemy, racism. That shameful UN resolution, number 3379 - has since been annulled. However, unfounded comparisons of that type, to which we, as Israelis, are constantly exposed (among them the attempt to make a link between Israel and genocide, and only recently, once again, with war crimes), not only do they confuse between partner and enemy; they also sabotage the ability of this Assembly to effectively fight the phenomenon of genocide. (Rivlin 2015)

Noam Chomsky, in his foreword to *The Politics of Genocide,* opines that "As for the term 'genocide,' perhaps the most honorable course would be to expunge it from the vocabulary until the day, if it ever comes, when honesty and integrity can become an 'emerging norm'" (Herman and Peterson 2011, 12).

It is time to stop accusing Israel of committing genocide. The false condemnation cheapens true accusations, cheapens true victims, cheapens NGOs that make the false accusations, cheapens international organizations that act on those false accusations, and it cheapens history.

# References

4thMedia. 2014. "Christof Lehmann." *4thmedia.org.* Accessed August 28, 2015. http://www.4thmedia.org/category/ christof-lehmann/.

Abunimah, Ali. 2008. "Israeli minister threatens "holocaust" as public demand ceasefire talks." *https://electronicintifada.net.* February 29. Accessed September 24, 2015. https://electronicintifada.net/content/israeli-minister-threatens-holocaust-public-demand-ceasefire-talks/7390.

Acheson, Dean. 1969. *Present at the Creation.* New York City: Norton.

ADL. 2015. "Anti-Semitic Conspiracies Continue In Aftermath Of Paris Attacks. "*ADL.org.* January 15. Accessed August 17, 2015. http://blog.adl.org/tags/ veterans-today.

AFP. 2014. "Erdogan says Israel attempting 'systematic genocide' in Gaza." *www.timesofisrael.com.* July 17. Accessed August 28, 2015. http://www.timesofisrael.com/erdogan-says-israel-atempting-systematic-genocide-in-gaza/.

Al-Jazeera. 2009. "Israel accused of Gaza 'genocide'." *http://www.aljazeera.com.* January 14. Accessed September 29, 2015. http://www.aljazeera.com/news/americas/ 2009/01/200911321467988347.html'.

Amit, Gish. 2010. "Salvage or Plunder? Israel's "Collection" of Private Palestinian Libraries in West Jerusalem." *Institute for Palestinian Studies.* Accessed August 17, 2015. http://www.palestine-studies.org/jps/fulltext/42473.

Andrews, Evan. 2014. "10 Things You May Not Know About Genghis Khan."History.com.April29.AccessedSeptember14,2016.http://www.history.com/news/history-lists/10-things-you-may-not-know-about-genghis-khan.

Annan, Kofi. 2004. "Throughout History Anti-Semitism Unique Manifestation of Hatred, Intolerance, Persecution says Secretary-General in Remarks to Headquarters Seminar." *UN.org.* June 21. Accessed August 23, 2015. http://www.un.org/press/en/2004/sgsm9375.doc.htm.

AP. 2006. "Another Day, Another Genocide." *http://normanfinkelstein.com.* August 29. Accessed October 15, 2015. http://normanfinkelstein.com/2006/08/29/another-day-another-genocide/.

Applebome, Peter. 2008. "Speech on the Mideast Brings Opinions to a Boil." *www.nytimes.com.* February 17. Accessed September 10, 2015. http://www.nytimes.com/ 2008/02/17/nyregion/17towns.html?_r=0.

Atzmon, Gilad. 2015. "JVP, Alison Weir And the Hatred of the White." *VeteransToday.* June 18. Accessed August 14, 2015. http://www.veteranstoday.com/ 2015/06/18/jvp-alison-weir-and-the-hatred-of-the-white/.

Bahour, Sam and Michael Dahan. 2004. "Genocide By Public Policy." *IfAmericansKnew.com.* May 19. Accessed August 14, 2015. http://www.ifamericansknew.org/ cur_sit/genocide.html.

Balaban, Oded. 2005. *Interpreting Conflict: Israeli-Palestinian Negotiations at Camp David.* New York City: Peter Lang.

Balakian, Peter. 2003. *The Burning Tigris.* New York City: HarperCollins.

Bancroft-Hinchey, Timothy. 2002. "Nobel Prize Winner compares Israel policy to Auschwitz." Pravdareport.com. March 27. Accessed January 10, 2016. http://www.pravdareport.com /news/russia/27-03-2002/36219-0/

Bard, Mitchell. 2015. "The Palestinian Refugees: History & Overview." Jewishvirtuallibrary.org. August. Accessed August 9, 2016. http://www.jewishvirtuallibrary.org/ jsource/History/refugees.html

Barghouti, Marwan Hassib. 2002. "Charges Against the State of Israel." *https://electronicintifada.ne.* October 3. Accessed September 24, 2015. https://electronicintifada.net/content/marwan-barghouti-presents-charge-sheet-against-state-israel-part-1-2/4133.

Barghouti, Omar. 2008. "Never against! European collusion in Israel's slow genocide." *https://electronicintifada.net.* January 21. Accessed Septmeber 24, 2015. https://electronicintifada.net/content/never-against-european-collusion-israels-slow-genocide/7309.

Barnett, David and Efraim Karsh. 2011. "Azzam's Genocidal Threat." *meforum.org.* Fall. Accessed August 26, 2015. http://www.meforum.org/3082/azzam-genocide-threat.

Bartrop, Paul. 2004. "Book Review." *Journal of Genocide Research* 269-271.

BBC. 2005. "Intifada toll 2000-2005." *http://news.bbc.co.uk.* February 8. Accessed September 24, 2015. http://news.bbc.co.uk/2/hi/middle_east/3694350.stm.

—. 2009. "Who are the Mid-East prisoners?" *BBC.co.UK.* November 26. Accessed September 9, 2015. http://news.bbc.co.uk/2/hi/middle_east/5211930.stm.

Beckerman, Gal. 2011. "Top Genocide Scholars Battle Over How To Characterize Israel's Actions." *Forward.com.* February 16. Accessed September 8, 2015. http://forward.com/news/135484/top-genocide-scholars-battle-over-how-to-character/.

Bickerton, Ian J. and Carla L. Klausner. 2010. *A History of the Arab-Israeli Conflict.* Boston: Prentice Hall.

Bigman, Petra Marquardt. 2014a. "Ali Abunimah's Orwellian Definition of Anti-Semitism." *http://brandeiscenter.com/.* May 2. Accessed September 24, 2015. http://brandeiscenter.com/blog/ali-abunimahs-orwellian-definition-of-anti-semitism/.

—. 2014b. "Anti-Israel Activists Thrilled by Abduction of Israeli Teens." *http://www.algemeiner.com.* June 15. Accessed September 24, 2015. http://www.algemeiner.com/2014/06/15/supporting-terrorism-and-bigotry-at-the-electronic-intifada/.

Biles, Peter. 2012. "Mau Mau massacre documents revealed." BBC.com. November 30. Accessed August 8, 2016. http://www.bbc.com/news/uk-20543140.

Blanchfield, Luisa. 2008. "The 2009 U.N. Durban Review Conference: Follow-Up to the 2001 U.N. World Conference Against Racism." *www.fas.org.* November 20. Accessed September 1, 2015. https://www.fas.org/sgp/crs/ row/RL34754.pdf.

Blighty. 2014. "Anti-Semitism in Britain, revisited." *Economist.com.* July 1. Accessed August 28, 2015. http://www.economist. com/ blogs/ blighty/2014/07/anti-semitism-britain-revisited.

Bloxham, Donald. 2005. "Rethinking the Armenian Genocide." *History Today* 28-30.

Boghossian, Paul. 2010. "The Concept of Genocide." *Journal of Genocide Research* 69-80.

Boghossian, Paul. 2015. "Academia.edu." *The Concept of Genocide.* August 13. Accessed August 13, 2015. https://www. academia. edu/241863/ The_Concept_of_Genocide.

Booth, William. 2014. "UN says 7 in 10 Palestinians killed in Gaza were civilians. Israel disagrees. August 29. Washingtonpost.com. Accessed August 9, 2016. https://www.washingtonpost.com/world/middle_east/ the-un-says-7-in-10-palestinians-killed-in-gaza-were-civilians-israel-disagrees/2014/08/29/44edc598-2faa-11e4-9b98-848790384093_ story.html.

Boren, Zachery. 2014. "Holocaust survivors and their descendants accuse Israel of 'genocide.'" *Independent.com* August 24. Accessed July 28, 2016. http://www.independent.co.uk/ news/ world/middle-east/holocaust-survivors-and-their-descendants-accuse-israel-of-genocide-9687994.html

Boyle, Francis A. 2000. "Palestine: Sue Israel for Genocide before the International Court of Justice!" *Journal of Muslim Minority Affairs* 161-166.

—. 2002. "Palestine, Palestinians and International Law." March 31. *Counterpunch.org.* Accessed January 17, 2016. http://www. counterpunch.org/2002/03/31/palestine-palestinians-and-international-law/

—. 2003. *Palestine, Palestinians and International Law.* Atlanta: Clarity Press.

—. 2011. *The Palestinian Right of Return under International Law.* Atlanta: Clarity Press.

—. 2013. "The Palestinian Genocide By Israel." *countercurrents.org.* August 30. Accessed August 18, 2015. http://www.countercurrents. org/boyle300813.htm.

Brandabur, A. Clare. 2008. "Roadmap to Genocide." *www. nobleworld. biz.* September. Accessed September 9, 2015. http://www.nobleworld. biz/nebulaarchive/ nebula53.html.

Brizon, Michael. 2014. "On the Meaning of Genocide." *NormanFinkelstein. com.* October 8. Accessed August 6, 2015. http://normanfinkelstein. com/2014/10/08/on-the-meaning-of-genocide/.

Brown, Anna. 2009. "Declaration of Genocide Scholars and Professionals on Israel and Palestine." IsraelGenocide.com. February 24. Accessed September 14, 2016. http://www.genocidetext.net/ israel_palestine02. htm

Buruma, Ian. 2001. "Blood Libel." *NewYorker.com.* April 1. Accessed August 3, 2015. http://www.newyorker.com/ magazine/2001/04/16/ blood-libel.

Camera. 2007a. "1948-1967: Jordanian Occupation of Eastern Jerusalem." *Camera.org.* Accessed August 25, 2015. http://www.sixdaywar.org/ content/ jordanianocuupationjerusalem.asp.

—. 2007b. "1967: Reunification of Jerusalem." *Camera.org.* Accessed August 25, 2015. http://www.sixdaywar.org /content/ReunificationJerusalem. asp.

—. 2007c. "Arab Threats Against Israel." *Camera.org.* Accessed August 26, 2015. http://www.sixdaywar.org/ content/threats.asp.

Carrim, Sabah. n.d. "Kuala Lumpur War Crimes Tribunal on Palestine: Judicial Biasness." *Academia.edu.* Accessed September 4, 2015. http://www.academia.edu/ 4466040/ Kuala_Lumpur_War_Crimes_ Tribunal_on_Palestine_Judicial_Biasness.

Carter, Stephen L. 2011. *The Violence of Peace.* New York City: Perseus Books Group (Beast Books).

Cesarani, David. 2000. "Finkelstein's final solution." *Timeshighereducation. co.uk.* August 4. Accessed August 18, 2015. https://www. timeshighereducation.co.uk/books/finkelsteins-final-solution/155953.article.

Charbonneau, Louis. 2014. "U.S. says glad 'noxious' U.N. rights envoy for Palestine leaving." *Reuters.com.* March 24. Accessed August 5, 2015. http://www.reuters.com/article/2014/03/24/us-palestinian-israel-un-idUSBREA2N1XU20140324.

Chehata, Hanan. 2010. "The Cultural Genocide of Palestine." *www. middleeastmonitor.com.* May 28. Accessed August 25, 2015. https:// www.middleeastmonitor.com/reports/by-dr-hanan-chehata.

CIA. 2016. "Middle East: Gaza Strip." CIA.gov. July 12. Accessed August 1. https://www.cia.gov/library/publications/ the- world-factbook/geos/gz.html.

Chomsky, Noam, and Ilan Pappé. 2010. *Gaza in Crisis: Reflections on Israel's War Against the Palestinians.* Chicago: Haymarket Books.

Christison, Kathleen and Bill Christison. 2006. "Does It Matter What You Call It?" *IfAmericansKnew.org.* November 27. Accessed August 15, 2015. http://www.ifamericansknew. org/cur_sit/genocideofpal. html.

Civil Rights Congress. 1951. "We Charge Genocide." *BlackPast.org.* December 17. Accessed August 13, 2015. http://www.blackpast. org/we-charge-genocide-historic-petition-united-nations-relief-crime-united-states-government-against.

Cook, William A. 2006. "www.counterpunch.org." *The Rape of Palestine.* January 7. Accessed August 14, 2015. http://www.counterpunch. org/2006/01/07/ the-rape-of-palestine/.

Cooper, Douglas A. 2011a. ""Genghis Khan With a Computer?"." *HuffingtonPost.com.* December 27. Accessed August 6, 2015. http://www.huffingtonpost.ca/douglas-anthony-cooper/israel-genocide_b_1146088.html.

—. 2011b. "Murder by the Numbers." *HuffingtonPost.com.* December 28. Accessed August 6, 2015.

http://www.huffingtonpost.ca/douglas-anthony-cooper/genocide-libel-ii_b_1146096.html

—. 2011c. "A Matter of Lies and Deaths." *HuffingtonPost.com.* December 29. Accessed August 6, 2015. http://www.huffingtonpost.ca/douglas-anthony- cooper/palestine-israel-genocide_b_1146105.html

—. 2011d. "Hatred Means Never Having to Say You're Sorry." *HuffingtonPost.com.* December 30. Accessed August 6, 2015. http://www.huffingtonpost.ca/douglas-anthony-cooper/israel-genocide_b_1169993.html

Cox, John M. 2011. *To Kill a People: Genocide in the 20th Century.* New York City: Pearson Hall.

Dalrymple, William. 2015. "The Great Divide: The violent legacy of Indian Partition." *The New Yorker,* June 29.

Davis, Patricia. 2014. "We Called It Genocide in Guatemala. Why Not in Gaza Too?" *http://fpif.org/called-genocide-guatemala-gaza/.* October 7. Accessed October 5, 2015. http://fpif.org/called-genocide-guatemala-gaza/.

Derfner, Larry. 2014. "Accusing Israel of 'genocide': Major fail." *972mag. com.* September 29. Accessed July 28, 2015. http://972mag.com/accusing-israel-of-genocide-major-fail/97099/.

Dickens, Charles. 1843. *A Christmas Carol.* London: Chapman & Hall.

Diplomat. 2012. "TheDiplomat.com." *Bush and Cheney on Trial.* May 20. Accessed August 17, 2015. http://thediplomat.com /2012/05/bush-and-cheney-on-trial/?allpages=yes.

Divest This. 2010. "Barghouti." *http://divestthis.com/2010/05/ barghouti. html.* May 14. Accessed September 24, 2015. http://divestthis.com/2010/05/barghouti.html.

Docker, John. 2003. "New history and the new catastrophe: Ilan Pappé, the new history and the question of Israeli genocide." *www. thefreelibrary.com.* August 1. Accessed September 21, 2015. http://www.thefreelibrary.com/ New+history+ and+the+new+catastrophe%3A+Ilan+Pappé,+the+new+history+and...-a0107894268.

—. 2004. "Raphael Lemkin's History of Genocide and Colonialism." *http://www.ushmm.org.* February 26. Accessed September 21, 2015.

http://www.ushmm.org/confront-genocide/speakers-and-events/ all-speakers-and-events/raphael-lemkins-history-of-genocide-and-colonialism.

—. 2010. "Raphaël Lemkin, creator of the concept of genocide: a world history perspective." *ANU.edu.* Accessed August 13, 2015. http:// press.anu.edu.au/apps/bookworm/view/ Humanities+Research+Vol+ XVI.+No.+2.+2010/5271/docker.xhtml#footnote-13493-71.

Docker, John, and Ned Curthoys. 2009. "The Gaza Massacre." *The Drum TV.* January 09. Accessed September 22, 2015. http://www.abc.net. au/news/2009-01-09/37828.

Doha, Lena Meari and Tanzeen. 2010. "An Interview with Critical Political Scientist Norman Finkelstein." *Chintaa.com.* October 13. Accessed August 6, 2015. http://www.chintaa.com/index.php/chinta/ showAerticle/72/english#sthash.VxwFkmst.dpuf.

Doubt, Keith. 2006. *Understanding Evil: Lessons from Bosnia.* New York City: Fordham University Press.

Dowty, Alan. 2005. *Israel/Palestine.* Cambridge: Polity Press.

Dvorsky, George. 2014. "Which countries do Americans perceive as their greatest enemies?" *io9.com.* February 21. Accessed August 13, 2015. http://io9.com/ which-countries-do-americans-perceive-as-their-greatest-1528098419.

Electronic Intifada. 2015. "genocide." *https://electronicintifada. net.* September 24. Accessed September 24, 2015. https:// electronicintifada.net/tags/ genocide?page=1.

End The Occupation. 2015. "Statement on Complaint Filed Regarding Alison Weir and If Americans Knew." *www.endtheoccupation.org.* July 16. Accessed September 9, 2015. http://www.endtheoccupation. org/article.php?id=4510.

ESCO. 2010. "Population Statistics." *ProCon.org.* September 17. Accessed August 15, 2015. http://israelipalestinian. procon.org/ view. resource.php?resourceID=000636.

Facing History. 2015. *Facing History.* Accessed August 12, 2016. https:// www.facinghistory.org/about-us.

Falk, Richard. 2007. "Slouching Toward a Palestinian Holocaust." *http://www.countercurrents.org*. July 7. Accessed September 24, 2015. http://www.countercurrents.org/falk070707.htm.

—. 2014. "Did Israel Commit Genocide in Gaza?." *The Gay Courier.* October 14. Accessed June 10, 2015. http://thegaycourier.blogspot. com/2014/10/did-israel-commit-genocide-in-gaza.html.

—. 2014b. "Former U.N. Special Rapporteur Richard Falk on the Legitimacy of Hope in the Palestinian Struggle." *http://www.democracynow.org*. October 21. Accessed September 24, 2015. http://www.democracynow. org/ 2014/10/21/ former_un_special_rapporteur_richard_falk.—. 2016. "Gazans Suffer, and the World Looks Away." Middleeasteye.net. January 29. Accessed August 12, 2016. http://www.middleeasteye. net/columns/while-gazans-suffer-world-moves-534564455

Fassed, Arjan El. 2003. "EU poll: "Israel poses biggest threat to world peace"." *Electronicintifada.net.* November 3. Accessed August 17, 2015. http://electronicintifada.net /content/eu-poll-israel-poses-biggest-threat-world-peace/4860.

Feiglin, Moshe. 2014. Letter to Israeli Prime Minister Netanyahu. https:// www.facebook.com/ MFeiglin/posts/695450140534104 translated and posted by Elke Booth. Accessed September 13, 2016. https:// www.facebook.com/ SmallPeopleAgainstBigGovernment/ photos/ pb.132550980096519.-2207520000.1421901250./ 823558350995775/? type=1&permPage=1.

Finkelstein, Norman G. 2000. *The Holocaust Industry: Reflections on the Exploitation of Jewish Suffering.* London: Verso Books.

Firsht, Naomi. 2015. "Southampton University cancels anti-Israel conference over 'safety concerns'." *thejc.com.* April 2. Accessed August 26, 2015. http://www.thejc.com/news/uk-news/133152/ southampton-university-cancels-anti-israel-conference-over-safety-concerns.

Forum, Ngo. 2001. "World Conference against Racism 2001 Declaration." *www.i-p-o.org.* September 3. Accessed September 2015, 2015. http://www.i-p-o.org/racism-ngo-decl.htm.

Forward. 2002. "Turkish Premier Recants Charge of Israeli Genocide." *The Forward.* New York City, April 12. Accessed September 3, 2015. http://search.proquest. com/ docview/367760158?accountid=8289.

FP Staff. 2015. "The Exchange: Joshua Oppenheimer and David Rieff on Genocide." *ForeignPolocy.com.* September 10. Accessed September 11, 2015. https://foreignpolicy.com /2015/09/10/the-exchange-joshua-oppenheimer-and-david-rieff-on-genocide-act-of-killing-look-of-silence/?utm_source=Sailthru&utm_medium=email&utm_campaign=New%20Campaign&utm_term=Flashpoints.

Frantzman, Seth J. 2008. "Review: The Ethnic Cleansing of Palestine." *www.meforum.org.* Spring. Accessed August 31, 2015. http://www.meforum.org/1886/the-ethnic-cleansing-of-palestine.

Frederick. 1986. *Hannah and Her Sisters, (United States: Orion Pictures Corporation, 1986).* Directed by Woody Allen. Performed by Frederick.

Freedman, Rosa. 2012. "THE UNITED NATIONS HUMAN RIGHTS COUNCIL: MORE OF THE SAME?" *Wisc.edu.* December 13. Accessed August 23, 2015. http://hosted.law.wisc.edu/wordpress/wilj/files/2014/01/Freedman_final_v2.pdf.

Frey, Rebecca Joyce. 2009. *Genocide and International Justice (Global Issues).* New York City: FOF

Friedman, Thomas L. 1982. "THE BEIRUT MASSACRE: THE FOUR DAYS." *http://www.nytimes.com.* September 25. Accessed October 16, 2015. http://www.nytimes.com/ 1982/09/26/world/the-beirut-massacre-the-four-days.html?pagewanted=all.

Galtung, Johan. 2012. "Sociocide, Palestine and Israel." *www.transcend.org.* October 8. Accessed August 16, 2015. https://www.transcend.org/tms/2012/10/sociocide-palestine-and-israel/.

Gardner, Frank. 2000. "Saddam threatens Israel." BBC.com. October 4. Accessed August 20, 2015. http://news.bbc.co.uk/2/hi/middle_east/956084.stm.

Genocide Convention. 1948. "Genocide Convention." *UN.org.* December 9. Accessed August 3, 2015. https://treaties.un.org/doc/Publication/UNTS/Volume%2078/ volume-78-I-1021-English.pdf.

Gheith, Jenny. 2004. "Exhibiting Politics: Palestinian-American Artist Emily Jacir Talks About her Work." *https://electronicintifada.net/content/exhibiting-politics-palestinian-american-artist-emily-jacir-talks-about-her-work/5295.* November 4. Accessed September 25, 2015. https://electronicintifada.net/content/exhibiting-politics-palestinian-american-artist-emily-jacir-talks-about-her-work/5295.

Goldberg, Chad Alan. 2005. "Politicide Revisited." *http://www.ssc.wisc.edu.* May. Accessed September 14, 2015. http://www.ssc.wisc.edu/~cgoldber/Web%20 Class/Goldberg2005a.pdf.

Goldhagen, Daniel Jonah. 2009. *Worse Than War: Genocide, Eliminationism, and the Ongoing Assault on Humanity.* New York City: Public Affairs.

Greenhouse, Abraham. 2012. "Russell Tribunal exposes futility of relying on UN." *https://electronicintifada.net.* October 9. Accessed September 24, 2015. https://electronicintifada.net/ blogs/abraham-greenhouse/russell-tribunal-exposes-futility-relying-un.

Grinberg, Lev. 2004. "Symbolic Genocide." *http://www.ginsburgh.net.* March 29. Accessed August 25, 2015. http://www.ginsburgh.net/textes/ Symbolic_Genocide _Grinberg.html.

Gutasli, Selcuk. 2009. "Norman Finkelstein: Israel is committing a holocaust in Gaza." *Zalman Today.* January 19. Accessed August 6, 2015. http://www.todayszaman.com/ interviews_norman-finkelstein-israel-is-committing-a-holocaust-in-gaza_164483.html.

Guttenplan, D. D. 2010. *The Holocaust on trial.* New York City: W. W. Horton & Company, Inc.

Ha'aretz. 2008. "Barak: Hamas Will Pay for Its Escalation in the South." *haaretz.co.* February 29. Accessed August 18, 2015. http://www.haaretz.com/news/barak-hamas-will-pay-for-its-escalation-in-the-south-1.240417.

Harff, Barbara. 1986. *Genocide as State Terrorism.* Edited by M. Stohl and G. A. Lopez. New York City: Greenwood Press.

HDOT. 2013. "Holocaust Denial and the 2000 Libel Trial in the U.K." *http://www.hdot.org.* Accessed October 2, 2015. http://www.hdot.org/en/trial/.

Herman, Edward S., and David Peterson. 2011. *The Politics of Genocide.* New York: Monthly Review Press.

Hollander, Ricki. 2009. "Anti-Jewish Violence in Pre-State Palestine/1929 Massacres." *Camera.org.* August 23. Accessed August 25, 2015. http://www.camera. org/index. asp?x_context=2&x_outlet=118&x_article=1691.

Holocaust Encyclopedia. 2015. "http://www.ushmm.org." *http://www. ushmm.org/wlc/en/article.php?ModuleId=10007316.* August 18. Accessed October 5, 2015. http://www.ushmm.org/wlc/en/article. php? ModuleId=10007316.

Horowitz, Adam and Philip Weiss. 2015. "Roundtable on the Palestinian solidarity movement and Alison Weir." *MondoWeiss.net.* August 12. Accessed August 14, 2015. http://mondoweiss.net/2015/08/ roundtable-palestinian-solidarity.

Hunter, Jane. 1987. *Israeli Foreign Policy: South Africa and Central America.* Boston: South End Press.

ICC-CPI. 2015. *What are War Crimes?* August 3. Accessed August 2015, 2015. http://www.icc-cpi.int/en_menus/icc/about%20the%20court/ frequently%20asked%20questions/Pages/13.aspx.

ICJ. 2007. "Application of the Convention on the Prevention and Punishment of the Crime of Genocide (Bosnia and Herzegovina v. Serbia and Montenegro)." *icj-cij.org.* February 26. Accessed August 18, 2015. http://www.icj-cij.org/docket/?sum=667&code=bhy&p1=3& p2=2&case=91&k=f4&p3=5.

ICPS. n.d. "Highest to Lowest - Prison Population Rate." *http://www. prisonstudies.org.* Accessed August 31, 2015. http://www.prisonstudies. org/highest-to-lowest/ prison_population_rate?field_region_taxonomy_ tid=All.

ICRC. 2015. "ICRC." *Rule 156. Definition of War Crimes.* August 4. Accessed August 15, 2015. https://www.icrc.org/ customary-ihl/eng/ docs/v1_cha_chapter44_rule156.

JewishVirtualLibrary. 1983. "The Kahan Commission of Inquiry." *www. jewishvirtuallibrary.org.* February 8. Accessed August 27, 2015. http:// www.jewishvirtuallibrary.org/ jsource/History/kahan.html.

Jochnowitz, George. ND. "Noam Chomsky - Extremist of the." *http://www.jochnowitz.net/*. Accessed August 11, 2015. http://www.jochnowitz.net/Essays/ExtremistLang.html.

Jones, Adam. 2006. *Genocide: A Comprehensive Introduction, 1st ed.* New York City: Routledge.

—. 2010. *Genocide: A Comprhensive Introduction, 2nd ed.* New York City: Routledge.

JVP. 2015. "Jewish Voice for Peace Statement on Our Relationship with Alison Weir." *https://jewishvoiceforpeace.org/*. July 15. Accessed September 9, 2015. https://jewishvoiceforpeace.org/jewish-voice-for-peace-statement-on-our-relationship-with-alison-weir/.

Kassel, Matthew. 2014. NY Times Runs Ad From Holocaust Survivors Condemning Israel, attacking Elie Wiesel." August 25. Accessed July 28, 2016. http://observer.com/2014/08/ny-times-runs-ad-from-holocaust-survivors-condemning-israel-attacking-elie-wiesel/

Katz, Samuel. 2002. Battle-ground: Fact and Fantasy in Palestine. New York City: Taylor Productions.

Khalek, Rania. 2014. "Israel's extermination of whole families in Gaza reflects genocidal impulse." *https://electronicintifada.net*. August 27. Accessed September 25, 2015. https://electronicintifada.net/ blogs/rania-khalek/israels-extermination-whole-families-gaza-reflects-genocidal-impulse.

Khalidi, Rashid. 2001. "The Palestinians and 1948: The Underlying Causes of Failure." In *The War for Palestine*, by Eugen Rogan and Avi Shlaim, edited by Eugen Rogan and Avi Shlaim, 12-36. Cambridge: Cambridge University Press.

—. 2006. *The Iron Cage.* Boston: Beacon Press.

Khalidi, Walid. 2001. *All That Remains: The Palestinian Villages Occupied and Depopulated by Israel in 1948, 3rd ed.* Washington DC: Institute for Palestine Studies.

Kiernan, Ben. 2007. *Blood and Soil.* Harrisonburg, VA: Yale University Press.

KLWCT. 2013. "The Kuala Lumpur War Crimes Tribunal." November 20-25. Accessed August 17, 2015. https://wikispooks.com/w/images/0/02/KL-IsraelWarCrimesJudgement.pdf.

Knew, If Americans. 2015. *www.facebook.com.* April 2. Accessed September 11, 2015. https://www.facebook.com/ permalink. php?story_fbid=10152775956324632&id=32975139631&comment_id =10152777965654632&offset=0&total_comments=12&comment_ tracking={%22tn%22%3A%22R%22}.

Kramer, David J. 2012. *Country Reports on Human Rights Practices for 2009.* Washington, DC: Joint Comittee Print.

Kramer, Martin. 2002. "Profs Condemn Israel in Advance." *MartinKramer.org.* Dwecember 20. Accessed August 18, 2015. http://www.martinkramer. org/ sandbox/2002/12/profs-condemn-israel-in-advance/.

Kuper, Leo. 1982. *Genocide: Its Political Use in the Twentieth Century.* New Haven: Yale University Press.

Kurth, Peter. 1990. *American Cassandra.* Boston: Little, Brown, and Company.

Legal Information Institute. n.d. "opinio juris." *www.law.cornell. edu.* Accessed September 7, 2015. https://www.law. cornell.edu/wex/ opinio_juris_international_law.

Lehmann, Christof. 2012. "30 Years After Sabra and Shatila the Genocide Continues with Impunity." *NSNBC. wordpress.com.* September 16. Accessed August 28, 2015. https://nsnbc. wordpress.com/2012/09/16/30-years-after-sabra-and-shatila-the-genocide-continues-with-impunity/.

Lendman, Stephen. 2011. *Commemorating The Palestinian Holocaust.* May 11. Accessed August 15, 2015. www.rense.com/general94/ comm.htm.

—. 2014a. "Israel - Guilty Of Genocidal High Crimes." *Rense.com.* September 27. Accessed August 5, 2015. http://www.rense.com/ general96/isguilt.html.

—. 2014b. "Israel: Palestinian Prisoner of Conscience Marwan Barghouti on Sham Peace Talks." *http://www.globalresearch.ca.* April 22. Accessed September 24, 2015. http://www.globalresearch.ca/ israel-palestinian-prisoner-of-conscience-marwan-barghouti-on-sham-peace-talks/5378713.

Levene, Mark. 2007. "Book Reviews." *Journal Of Genocide Research* 675-681.

—. 2010. "Genocide." *www.gendersidetext.net.* August 13. Accessed August 12, 2015. http://www.genocidetext.net/.

Lipstadt, Deborah. 1993. *Denying the Holocaust.* New York City: Free Press.

Livik, Adam. 2012. "Guardian Praises Anti-Semitic Site "CounterPunch" as Progressive." *http://www.algemeiner.com.* July 25. Accessed August 14, 2015. http://www.algemeiner.com/2012/07/25/ guardian-praises-anti-semitic-site-counterpunch-as-progressive/.

Lozowick, Yaacov. 2003. *Right To Exist.* New York: Anchor Books.

Lungen, Paul. 2008. "Canada Opposes Anti-Israel Resolutions at UN." Cjnews.com. April 2. Accessed December 21, 2015. http://www. cjnews.com/news/canada- opposes-anti-israel-resolutions-un.

Machover, Daniel. 2015. "Sociocide – promoting the debate so law meets reality?" *www.russelltribunalonpalestine.com.* Accessed August 16, 2015. http://www. russelltribunalonpalestine. com/en/ daniel-machover-2.

Mallison, W. Thomas and Sally V. Mallison. 1986. *The Palestine Problem in International Law and World Order.* Essex: Longman Group.

Malone, Linda A. 1985. "The Kahan Report, Ariel Sharon and the Sabra-Shatilla Massacres in Lenbanon." *WM.edu.* Accessed August 19, 2015. http:// scholarship.law.wm.edu/cgi/ viewcontent.cgi?article=16 06&context=facpubs.

Mamdani, Mahmood. 2007. "The Politics of Naming: Genocide, Civil War, Insurgency." *London Review of Books.* March 8. Accessed September 23, 2015. http://www.lrb.co.uk /v29/n05/mahmood-mamdani/ the-politics-of-naming-genocide-civil-war-insurgency.

Masalha, Nur. 2003. *The Politics of Denial : Israel and the Palestinian Refugee Problem.* London: Pluto Press.

McCarthy, Justin. 2001. "Palestine Population: During The Ottoman And The British Mandate Periods." *http://www. palestineremembered. com.* September 8. Accessed September 24, 2015. http://www.

palestineremembered. com/Acre/Palestine-Remembered/Story559. html.

McGreal, Chris. 2004. "World court tells Israel to tear down illegal wall." *TheGuardian.com.* July 9. Accessed August 2015, 2015. http://www. theguardian.com/world/2004/jul/10/israel3.

MEMO. 2014. "Census reveals Palestinians to surpass 12 million by the end of 2014." *middleeastmonitor.org.* December 30. Accessed August 25, 2015. https://www.middleeastmonitor. com/news/ middle-east/16071-census-reveals-palestinians-to-surpass-12-million-by-the-end-of-2014.

—. 2014. "Fidel Castro accuses Israel of practicing genocide against Palestinians." *Memo.org.* August 6. Accessed August 31, 2015. https:// www.middleeastmonitor.com/news/ americas/13283-fidel-castro-accuses-israel-of-practicing-genocide-against-palestinians.

Morris, Benny. 2008a. "Using Bombs to Stave Off War." Nytimes.com. July 18. Accessed January 10, 2016. http://www.nytimes.com/2008/07/18/ opinion/ 18morris.html?_r=0.

—. 2008b. "Israel and Iran: A Response to James Petras." *e-ir.info.* July 31. Accessed August 28, 2015. http://www.e-ir.info /2008/07/31/ israel-and-iran-a-response-to-james-petras/.

—. 2010. "The 1948 War Was an Islamic Holy War." *meforun.org.* Summer. Accessed August 25, 2015. http://www.meforum. org/ 2769/ benny-morris-1948-islamic-holy-war.

—. 2011. "Liar as Hero." *www.newrepublic.com.* March 17. Accessed Augst 18, 2015. http://www.newrepublic.com/ article/books/ magazine/85344/ilan-Pappé-sloppy-dishonest-historian.

Moses, Dirk. 2004. "Genocide and Settler Society in Australian History." *dirkmoses.com.* Accessed September 8, 2015. http://www.dirkmoses. com/uploads/7/3/8/2/7382125/01-ch1moses.pdf.

—. 2006. "Why the Discipline of 'Genocide Studies' Has Trouble Explaining How Genocides End?" *How Genocides End.* December 22. Accessed August 4, 2015. http://howgenocidesend.ssrc.org/Moses/.

—. 2013. "Genocide." *www.australianhumanitiesreview.org.* Accessed September 8, 2015. http://www.australianhumanitiesreview.org/archive/Issue-November-2013/AHR55_2_Moses.pdf.

Ndugga-Kabuye and Rachel Gilmer. 2016. "Invest-Divest." Accessed August 7, 2016. https://policy.m4bl.org.

NGO Monitor. 2012. "Russel Tribunal on Palestine." October 3. Accessed November 12, 2015. http://www.ngo-monitor.org/ngos/russell_tribunal_on_palestine/

Open Democracy. 2015. "Singling Out Israel: A Perspective from the Left." *Open Democracy*, June 3. doi: .

OSAPG. 2015. "Legal Definition of Genocide." *UN.org.* August 6. Accessed August 6, 2015. http://www.un.org/en/ preventgenocide/adviser/pdf/osapg_analysis_framework.pdf.

Özsu, Umut. 2013. "'A thoroughly bad and vicious solution': humanitarianism, the World Court, and the modern origins of population transfer." *London Review of International Law* 99-127.

Pappé, Ilan. 2006a. *The Ethnic Cleansing of Palestine.* Oxford: One World.

—. 2006b. "Genocide in Gaza." *https://electronicintifada.net.* September 2. Accessed September 24, 2015. https://electronicintifada.net/content/genocide-gaza/6397.

—. 2007. "Palestine 2007: Genocide in Gaza, Ethnic Cleansing in the West Bank." *https://electronicintifada.net/.* January 11. Accessed September 24, 2015. https://electronicintifada.net/content/palestine-2007-genocide-gaza-ethnic-cleansing-west-bank/6673.

—. 2013. "When Israeli denial of Palestinian existence becomes genocidal." *https://electronicintifada.net.* April 20. Accessed September 24, 2015. https://electronicintifada.net/content/when-israeli-denial-palestinian-existence-becomes-genocidal/12388.

Perry, Nigel. 2004. "Time to put the US media on trial for complicity in genocide?" *https://electronicintifada.net.* June 4. Accessed Septemeber 24, 2015. https://electronicintifada.net/content/time-put-us-media-trial-complicity-genocide/5118.

Petras, James. 2002. "Palestine: the final solution and Jose Saramago." *Petras.lahaine.org*. April 2. Accessed January 10, 2016. http://petras. lahaine.org/?p=124

—. 2003. "The war and premeditated genocide: What is at stake?" *rebelion.org*. February 12. Accessed August 28, 2015. http://www. rebelion.org/hemeroteca/ petras/english/war160203.htm.

—. 2008a. "The New York Times: Making Nuclear Extermination Respectable." *GlobalResearch.ca.* July 30. Accessed August 28, 2015. http://www.globalresearch.ca/ the-new-york-times-making-nuclear-extermination-respectable/9711.

—. 2008b. "Racism and Genocide: Lies of our Times." *E- InternationalRelations.info*. August 6. Accessed January 10, 2016. http://www.e-ir.info/2008/08/06/racism-and- genocide-lies-of-our-times/.—. 2014. "Israeli Genocide and its Willing Accomplices." *petras. org.* November 8. Accessed August 28, 2015. http://petras.lahaine. org/?p=1998&print=1.

Post, Jerusalem. 2015. "Grand mufti: There was never a Jewish Temple on Temple Mount." *http://www.jpost.com.* October 27. Accessed October 27, 2015. http://www.jpost.com/Arab-Israeli-Conflict/Grand-mufti-There-was-never-a-Jewish-Temple-on-Temple-Mount-430131.

Powell, Colin. 2001. "World Conference Against Racism." *WWW.State. gov.* September 3. Accessed September 1, 2015. http://2001-2009. state.gov/secretary/ former/powell/remarks/2001/4789.htm.

Pro-Con. 2009. "41 Maps covering 5000 Years of History. *Procon.org.* July 2. Acessed December 1, 2016. http://israelipalestinian.procon. org/view.resource.php?resourceID=000642.

Rashed, Hafia, and and Damien Short. 2012. "Genocide and settler co-lonialism: can a Lemkin-inspired genocide perspective aid our un-derstanding of the Palestinian situation?" *The International Journal of Human Rights* 1142-69.

Quigley, John. 2005. *The Case for Palestine.* Durham: Duke University Press.

Rashed, Haifa, Damient Short, and John Docker. 2014. "Nakba Memoricide: Genocide Studies and the Zionist/Israeli Genocide of Palestine." *Holy Land Studies* 1-23.

Ratner, Michael, interview by Jessica Desvarieux. 2014. "UN's Investigation of Israel Should Go Beyond War Crimes to Genocide." *The Ratner Report.* (July 27). Accessed September 25, 2015. http://therealnews. com/t2/ index. php?option=com_content&task=view&id=31&Itemid= 74&jumival=12155&updaterx=2014-07-28+11%3A42%3A40.

Reese, Frederick. 2013. "Anniversary Of The Sabra And Shatila Massacres In Lebanon Passes Largely Unnoticed." *friendsoflebanon.org.* September 24. Accessed August 17, 2015. http://friendsoflebanon. org/archives/1622.

Rivlin, Reuvin. 2015. "President Rivlin addresses UN General Assembly: International Holocaust Remembrance Day." *mfa.gov.il.* January 28. Accessed August 3, 2015. http://mfa.gov.il/MFA/AboutIsrael/ History/Holocaust/Pages/President-Rivlin-addresses-UN-General-Assembly-International-Holocaust-Remembrance-Day-2015.aspx.

Rochester, U of. 2015. "Distinguished Visiting Humanist Program." *www. rochester.edu.* Accessed August 11, 2015. https://www.rochester. edu/college/humanities/ events/visiting-humanist/index.html.

Romirowsky, Asaf, and Efriam Karsh. 2015. "The Politicization of Middle East Studies." *TheAmericanInterest.com.* September 18. Accessed September 20, 2015. http://www.the-american-interest. com/2015/09/18/the-politicization-of-middle-east-studies/.

RToP. 2012. "New York Session – October 6 – 7 2012." *Russell Tribunal on Palestine.* October 12. Accessed September 14, 2015. http://www. russelltribunal onpalestine.com/en/sessions/future-sessions.

—. 2014. "The Russell Tribunal on Palestine." *http://www.europarl. europa.eu/.* September 25. Accessed August 11, 2015. http://www. europarl.europa.eu/ meetdocs/ 2014_2019/documents/dplc/dv/ summary-of-findings_/summary-of-findings_en.pdf.

Sabien. 2015. "6. Humpty Dumpty." *Sabien.org.* Accessed August 31, 2015. http://sabian.org/ looking_glass6.php.

Said, Edward. 2001. "Afterword." In *The War for Palestine*, by Eugene L. Rogan and Avi Shlaim, 206-219. Cambridge: Cambridge University Press.

Schabas, William. 2006. *A Legal Distinction between 'Genocide' 'War Crimes' and 'Crimes Against Humanity'.* Accessed August 4, 2015.

A Legal Distinction between 'Genocide' 'War Crimes' and 'Crimes Against Humanity'.

—. 2009. *Genocide in International Law.* 2nd. Cambridge: Cambridge University Press.

—. 2010 Interview by John. "A Legal Distinction between 'Genocide' 'War Crimes' and 'Crimes Against Humanity'." *A Legal Distinction between 'Genocide' 'War Crimes' and 'Crimes Against Humanity' - William Schabas.* (October 4). Accessed August 31, 2015. https://www.youtube.com/watch?v=_PMP2ckW6Fw.

—. 2014. "Convention on the Prevention and Punishment of the Crime of Genocide." *UN.org.* Accessed September 14, 2015. http://legal.un.org/avl/ha/cppcg/cppcg.html.

Sedan, Gil. 2001. "Mideast cease-fire doesn't extend into cyberspace." *http://www.jweekly.com.* June 29. Accessed September 24, 2015. http://www.jweekly.com/article/full/ 15958/mideast-cease-fire-doesn-t-extend-into-cyberspace/.

Sharkov, Damien. 2014. "Turkish Prime Minister Accuses Israel of Genocide as Diplomats Are Pulled Out." *Newsweek.com.* July 18. Accessed August 23, 2015. http://europe.newsweek.com/turkish-prime-minister-accuses-israel-genocide-diplomats-are-pulled-out-259776.

Shaw, Martin. 2007. *What is Genocide?* Cambridge: Polity Press.

—. 2010. "Palestine in an International Historical Perspective on Genocide." *Holy Land Sudies* 1-25.

—. 2013. "Palestine and Genocide: An International Historical Perspective Revisited." *Holy Land Studies* 1-7.

Sher, Trevor. 2015. *The Israeli Genocide Myth.* March 16. Accessed August 5, 2015. http://blogs.timesofisrael.com/the-genocide-myth/.

Smith, Jordan Michael. 2015. "An Unpopular Man." *NewRepublic.com.* July 7. Accessed September 2, 2015. http://www.newrepublic.com/article/122257/unpopular-man-norman-finkelstein-comes-out-against-bds-movement.

Sontag, Deborah. 2001. "Suicide Bomber Kills 3 Israelis After Deaths of 6 Palestinians." *NYTimes.com.* March 5. Accessed September 10,

2015. http://www.nytimes.com/2001/03/05/ world/suicide-bomber-kills-3-israelis-after-deaths-of-6-palestinians.html.

Stand4facts. 2005. "If Americans Knew: Profile." *Stand4facts.org.* Accessed August 15, 2015. http://www.discoverthenetworks. org/ Articles/ ifamericans. html.

Stein, Leslie. 2011. "Rewriting Israel's History." *Shofar: An Interdisciplinary Journal of Jewish Studies* 129-139.

Stoett, Peter J. 2000. *The Genocide Reader.* Edited by Marnie J. McCuen. Hudson, Wisconsin: Gary McCuen Puplications.

Swarns, Rachel L. 2001. "Racism Walkout Overview: US and Israelis Quit Racism Talks over Denunciation." *NYTimes.com.* September 4. Accessed 1 2015, September. http://www.nytimes.com/ 2001/09/04/ world/racism-walkout-overview-us-israelis-quit-racism-talks-over-denunciation.html.

Tatz, Colin. 2003. *With intent to Destroy.* London: Verso.

Tessler, Mark. 2009. *A History of the Israeli-Palestinian Conflict, 2nd ed.* Bloomington: Indiana Univesity Press.

Tharoor, Ishaan. 2015. "Israle's new justice minister considers all Palestinians to be 'the enemy.'" Washingtonpost.com. May 7. Accessed August 9, 2016. https://www.washingtonpost. com/ news/ worldviews/wp/2015/05/07/israels-new-justice-minister-considers-all-palestinians-to-be-the-enemy/

The Financial Express. 2014. "Ershad Wants AL to Protest Israeli Genocide." *The Financial Express.* Dhaka, August 7. Accessed September 3, 2015. http://print.thefinancialexpress-bd.com/2014/08/07/49105.

Thiessen, Marc A. 2015. "Who is the world's worst serial abuser of human rights, according to the UN Human Rights Commission? Israel." *American Enterprise Institute.* June 25. Accessed August 27, 2015. https://www.aei.org/ publication/who-is-the-worlds-worst-serial-abuser-of-human-rights-according-to-the-un-human-rights-commission-israel/.

Times, New York. 2000. "Sharon Touches a Nerve, and Jerusalem Explodes." *http://www.nytimes.com.* September 29. Accessed

September 9, 2015. http://www.nytimes.com/ 2000/09/29/ world/29ISRA.html.

Totten, Samuel and William S. Parsons, ed. 2013. *Centuries of Genocide.* New York City: Routledge.

Tsilfidis, Aris. 2015. "The Exchange of Populations: Greece and Turkey." *http://pontosworld.com.* Accessed September 18, 2015. http://pontosworld.com/index.php/pontus/history/ articles/295-the-exchange-of-populations-greece-and-turkey.

UN. 1947. "UNGA resolution 181." *UN.org.* November 29. Accessed August 25, 2015. http://unispal.un.org/UNISPAL. NSF/0/7F0AF2BD8 97689B785256C330061D253.

—. 2008. "Human Rights Council Elects Advisory Committee Members and Approves a Number of Special Procedures Mandate Holders." *http://unispal.un.org.* March 26. Accessed August 12, 2016. http://www.webcitation.org/5dViuhEdA

UN Watch. 2013. "U.S. Rep to UNHRC: Richard Falk "unfit to serve"." *http://blog.unwatch.org.* April 24. Accessed September 28, 2015. http://blog.unwatch.org/index.php/2013/04/26/u-s-rep-to-unhrc-richard-falk-unfit-to-serve/.

UNGA. 1946. "The Crime of Genocide." *UN.org.* December 11. Accessed August 2015, 2015. http://daccess-dds-ny.un.org/doc/RESOLUTION/ GEN/NR0/ 033/47/ IMG/NR003347.pdf?OpenElement.

—. 1948. "Convention on the Prevention and Punishment of the Crime of Genocide." *UN.org.* December 9. Accessed August 17, 2015. https:// treaties.un.org/doc/ Publication/UNTS/ Volume%2078/volume-78-I-1021-English.pdf.

—. 1982. "A/RES/37/123." *UN.org.* December 16. Accessed August 31, 2015. http://www.un.org/documents/ ga/res/37/a37r123.htm.

UNHRC. 2006. "Human Rights Council Discusses Situation in Occupied Palestinian Territories in Context of Follow-up of its Decisions." *UN.org.* September 29. Accessed August 5, 2015. http://unispal. un.org/UNISPAL.NSF/0/ BB9A9A833D273EC0852571FB0046D475.

Wadi, Ramona. 2014. "TheU.N.'s Endorsement of Israel's Genocidal Intent." Mintpressnews.com. August 6. Accessed August 10, 2016. http://www.mintpressnews.com/the-u-n-s-endorsement-of-israels-genocidal-intent/194928/

Webre, Alfred Lambremont. 2013. "How and why the Kuala Lumpur War Crimes Tribunal was destabilized." *http://exopolitics.blogs.com.* November 10. Accessed September 30, 2015. http://exopolitics.blogs.com/ breaking_news/2013/11/how-and-why-the-kuala-lumpur-war-crimes-tribunal-was-destabilized.html.

Weir, Alison. 2003. "Death Threats in Berkeley." *IfAmericansknew.org.* October 19. Accessed August 15, 2015. http://www.ifamericansknew.org/about_us/ dt_editorial.html.

—. 2004. "Censored: Israel and Palestine." *IfAmericansKnew.* Accessed August 15, 2015. http://www.ifamericansknew.org/media/sides.html.

—. 2013. "Anti-Semisim Tag Used as Israeli Ploy." Argus Leader. October. Accessed August 2, 2016. http://www.ifamericansknew.org/media/argus.html.

—. 2014. *Against Our Better Judgment.* CreateSpace Independent Publishing Platform.

—. 2015a. "Please help us overcome the accusations." *IfAmericansKnew. org.* August. Accessed August 15, 2015. http://www.ifamericansknew.org/about_us/accusations.html.

—. 2015b. "Dear Friends." *IfAmericansKnew.org.* May 20. Accessed August 15, 2015. http://secure.campaigner.com/Campaigner/Public/t.show?8a6tj--4asmj-b38cgy8&_v=2.

—. 2015c. "Response to US Campaign's accusations against If Americans Knew." *www.IfAmericansKnew.com.* September 27. Accessed September 28, 2015. http://www. ifamericansknew.org/about_us/accusations.html#fifteen.

—. n.d. "Dear Friends." *If Americans Knew.* Accessed September 14, 2015. http://secure.campaigner.com/Campaigner/ Public/t.show?850gx--44po0-b38cgy5&_v=2.

Westmoreland, Mark Ryan. 2015. *Crisis of representation: Experimental documentary in postwar Lebanon.* Ann Arbor: Proquest.

Wilder, David. 2006. "An open letter to Swedish Ambassador: The Honorable Robert Rydberg." *www.hebron.com.* November 22. Accessed August 14, 2015. http://www.hebron.com/english/article.php?id=294.

Williams Jr., Nick B. and Daniel Williams. 1990. "Iraq Threatens Israel With Use of Nerve Gas : Mideast: Leader denies nuclear capability but says he would destroy 'half' his adversary if attacked." *LATimes.com.* April 3. Accessed August 26, 2015. http://articles.latimes.com/1990-04-03/news/mn-702_1_gas-attack.

Zaman. 2014. "Erdoğan says Israel is committing 'genocide' in Gaza." *www.todayszaman.com.* July 24. Accessed August 28, 2015. http://www.todayszaman.com/anasayfa_erdogan-says-israel-is-committing-genocide-in-gaza_353973.html.

Zieve, Tamara. 2012. "This Week In History: Masses protest Sabra, Shatila." *JPost.com.* September 23. Accessed August 19, 2015. http://www.jpost.com/ Features/In-Thespotlight/This-Week-In-History-Masses-protest-Sabra-Shatila.

Zuesse, Eric. 2000. *Why the Holocaust happened.* Superiorbooks.com (defunct?). —. 2015. "Massive News-Suppression that has become History- Suppression." Countercurrents.org. April 1. Accessed September 12, 2015. http://www.countercurrents.org/ zuesse010415.htm

www.ingramcontent.com/pod-product-compliance
Lightning Source LLC
Chambersburg PA
CBHW060309290526
45789CB00001B/451